MYSTICAL STITCHES

Embroidery *for* Personal Empowerment *and* Magical Embellishment

CHRISTI JOHNSON

PHOTOGRAPHY BY BRAD OGBONNA

Storey Publishing

This book is dedicated to anyone who's ever been told they aren't creative,
or that their art isn't good enough.

The mission of Storey Publishing is to serve our customers by
publishing practical information that encourages
personal independence in harmony with the environment.

Edited by Liz Bevilacqua
Art direction and book design by Alethea Morrison
Text production by Liseann Karandisecky
Indexed by Samantha Miller

Cover and interior photography by © Brad Ogbonna
Additional photos courtesy of Christi Johnson, 7, 29, 55, 82, 103, 107, 110–114, 144, 149; Mars Vilaubi © Storey Publishing, LLC,
    vi, vii, 5, 17, 20, 28, 29, 32, 39, 47, 55 (background), 56–80, 83–102, 104, 105, 107, 132, 133, 143, 155
Illustrations by © Nina Chakrabarti, except for Chapter 7 by Ilona Sherratt © Storey Publishing, LLC

Storey books are available at special discounts when purchased in bulk for premiums and sales promotions as well as for fund-raising or educational use. Special editions or book excerpts can also be created to specification. For details, please call 800-827-8673, or send an email to sales@storey.com.

Storey Publishing
210 MASS MoCA Way
North Adams, MA 01247
storey.com

Printed in China through Asia Pacific Offset
10 9 8 7 6 5 4 3 2 1

Library of Congress Cataloging-in-Publication Data on file

Contents

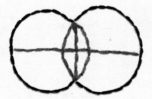

FOREWORD

When I was writing *Native Funk & Flash*, I was delighted to find people working with scissors, needle, and thread who had immense flair and virtually no prior skill with embroidery. One woman, for example, had only a vision and desire for a cloak with red velvet along the bottom edging. She took a worn and torn old thing, stitched multicolored patches onto it with long running stitches, added red velvet on the back, and we photographed it. People loved it! You have permission—with only yourself to please.

Mystical Stitches is the perfect companion to get you on your way and pull you out of any snag in your imagination. This book will be a best friend in your early days while you try out new stitches, discovering which ones provide a rhythm you most enjoy and a look that pleases you. And later, it will help you discover stitches for special effects or give your creativity a boost when you want a new idea to bloom.

Christi Johnson is an all-out stitchery witch. She undercuts your fears of not being good enough and breaks through the limiting beliefs that you are not creative or not an artist. The truth is, by the time you are old enough to pick up a needle you've already put some creative juices into simply living. All you need to get started with embroidery is a threaded needle in your hand. Once you stick that needle into fabric, the magic can begin. Stitch by stitch you'll start creating, and you'll soon discover a magical path. There are so many wonderful ways to manipulate those threads through twists and turns of the needle, and Christi's guidance makes the journey interesting, fun, and productive.

Christi also understands the spiritual value of slowing down and focusing. As a kind of meditation and practice, embroidery has calmed me through some pretty rough patches. The rhythmic, watchful, and even pace, studded with little snags to be successfully handled, offers me a sense of competence, relaxation, and productivity all at once. I have an embroidery-inspired mantra, "Accepting What Is," on my refrigerator as a recipe for happiness!

I am delighted to recommend Christi's work and words to you for your own exploration of self through art, especially the art of the hands, one careful stitch after another.

Alexandra Jacopetti Hart
author of *Native Funk & Flash*

Native Funk & Flash

The Discovery of Creative Liberation

When I was a child, the public library held the keys to my personal freedom. Before we'd even make it home, I was eagerly flipping through page after flimsy page of black-and-white instructions, past photos laying out precise techniques and displaying slightly antiquated tools and materials organized in a most aesthetically pleasing fashion.

Then came the holy grail:

The feeling of thick, glossy pages sparking the realization of everything I'd been waiting for. Full-color plates practically popping out of the spine, rich with images of undulating forms created in vibrant fibers. Maybe the projects were wearable or usable, maybe they were just works of art to be admired for their beauty. These plates lit up my childhood, and I checked out piles of the oldest craft books I could find in the library to bring home and pore over every detail.

There were certainly plenty of full-color books in the craft section of the library by the time I was old enough to read, but their pages didn't express the same feeling of freedom and liberation I found in books written in the 1960s and '70s. Contemporary craft books seemed to bring with them the presumption that you weren't capable of creating your own designs. They spelled out each project step-by-step with the exact colors and supplies you needed to re-create the designs pictured. These books stifled my creativity and seemed to further emphasize my lack of skills. The wild styles of books written a few decades earlier gave me something to dream toward; they seemed to recognize my wish to be free from structure while still supporting me through learning a new skill or technique.

I never lost that desire for ultimate liberation, and from these humble craft books of a past era emerged an evolving association between the freedom found in an artistic practice and the freedom found in a spiritual practice.

I love the vibrant freedom of the stitches in books from the 1960s and '70s. The style is unintimidating and joyful.

Further Liberation through Meditation

My interest in meditation began as a desperate need to find grounding amid the stress of working in the rapidly paced fashion industry. I quickly recognized how effective this practice was at helping me find acceptance with all that is in every arena of my life. As meditative contemplation permeated all of my experiences, it began to make its way into my artwork. Art making is a lifelong practice I've also found to be a highly effective means of calming the body and focusing the mind.

My creations evolved from attempts at literal representations of the world around me to a translation of concepts and images gathered during periods of quiet introspection. The symbols dancing behind closed eyelids became the new subject of my work, combined with an interest in recycling and reusing discarded fabrics when possible. The exploration of available materials, and attempts to expand the possibilities of technique, continues to drive my practice as I search not for perfection but for a feeling of personal freedom.

This book presents a path for your own creative liberation through the study of embroidery. More than simply a series of projects to complete, it is a way of thinking about your own artistic process as a magical ritual—and explores how this perspective can inform your approach to the rest of your life. I offer projects, patterns, and colors as creative inspiration; feel free to use these as jumping-off points to spread your wings and explore what works for you.

You're invited to embrace everything from beauty to sadness, express through fibers the grace found in accepting what is, and explore future possibilities of personal transformation through the stitching of dreams and intentions.

Christi Johnson

INTENTION

To view the world from a mystical perspective is to hold all things in reverence, honoring the divine essence in all forms of life. The emergence of an idea out of nowhere, the manifestation of inner visions into the outer world, the impact of viewing a work of art—these elements of the creative process that science cannot explain possess a truly mystical quality. Every day, we are confronted with the choice of conforming to the ways of society or courageously creating a life for ourselves. The more we become familiar with our ability to manifest change in the physical world through creative activities, the more empowered we are to manifest change in our lives.

The Magic in the Creative Act

Our culture tends to consider the creative act as a means to an end, the end being "good" art. Many of our early creative expressions are wounded by well-intentioned teachers, parents, or friends who have a negative, judgmental, or uninterested reaction to our artwork. When I began leading embroidery workshops, I realized that many of us hold this creative wound and will recoil at the sight of a paintbrush or chalk pastel, but embroidery tends to be free of these judgmental associations, making it an ideal avenue for exploration.

The creative freedom accessed through embroidery allows an opportunity to express ourselves free from the perceived need to make "good" art. And it helps us access this creativity in other areas of our life that may have grown stagnant or committed to the "rational" course or the way things "should" be. Creativity is at its core *irrational* in its act of bringing into being what did not already exist.

Both the creative act and the desire to connect with higher powers hold within them the possibility for personal transformation. When we create mystical stitches, the line between our own creative essence and the greater creative essence of divine powers is blurred as we consider ways to connect these two experiences. By sparking our imagination with symbols that speak to the deepest parts of ourselves, we begin to stitch together a new world in which to exist.

The creative process is not simply about what is being made; it's an entirely mystical process that teaches us how to move between the internal world of the soul and the physical world outside. All that is illuminated at the crossing of this bridge happens first in making a piece of art and, eventually, through the shaping of existence itself. By allowing ourselves to engage with our own creative process, we become more and more familiar with bringing our dreams into reality.

The Power of Symbols

Long before written language, our species learned to communicate through symbols. As children, we learn to identify images before we can speak. And when we reach for knowledge beyond our own culture, symbols allow us to transcend the limitations of language. Imagery as the basis of communication applies to our internal workings as well. The field of depth psychology posits that our brains work from two distinct areas: the rational, intellectual method of the conscious mind, and the less understood subconscious mind, which seems to run on instinctual and intuitive processes. Our conscious mind may choose language as its primary voice, but, as is evident in the wild imaginal realm of our dreams, our subconscious mind prefers to speak in symbols, of both personal and universal associations.

The divine meanings expressed through visual forms often travel across time and cultures, as the essential meanings of many symbols share similarities throughout the history of humankind. By witnessing the cycles of our galaxy and our lives on Earth, many ancient civilizations began to notice greater divine patterns taking shape and influencing our existence. These divine patterns have evolved into studies such as astronomy, astrology, and to some extent biology, though the idea that there's a greater power acting through these forms was put aside within the past few centuries.

These greater divine patterns are where *correspondences* come in. By working with images and forms that correspond to the feeling and emotion we'd like to bring about in our own life, we are acting upon the idea that all things are interrelated in this tapestry of existence. We can speak to our subconscious through the symbols in our immediate world, and get the subconscious aligned with the conscious mind.

Think of it like this: Our conscious mind is the tip of the iceberg, above the water, saying, "Yes, I'd like to go that way!" Meanwhile, the subconscious, the giant chunk of ice below the surface, is the rudder steering the ship. Our subconscious language, the underwater language, is one of archetypes and symbols. By creating talismans—condensations of meaning through images—we can show the subconscious which direction we'd like to go in the language it understands.

Our subconscious is full of archaic associations that have likely been passed down through our ancestors in the same way our physical traits have. This

subconscious landscape of symbolic associations—our psyches, emotional tendencies, instincts, and intuitions—may be quite similar to our ancient ancestors'. We can continue to access this part of our brains through working with symbols: images that travel throughout time and space, eternal and omnipresent.

Imagine you're in a different country where you don't speak the language. If you try to ask for directions, words will fail you. But if you pull out maps or pictures, you can get your intention across and move on with your travels. This is how talismans work. They send messages inward to our deep internal desires and out to the cosmos, intertwined in a divine pattern.

Accessing the depths of the subconscious through symbols requires a willingness to believe in magic, to believe in the ability to enact change and bring new forms or possibilities into being. Open yourself up to these realms by allowing yourself to believe the unbelievable—even if just for a minute.

What Is a Talisman?

An object is considered to be transformed into an enchanted talisman when we call upon natural energies to charge it with our desired intention. The powers of the natural world, our own personal power, and cosmic powers—this meeting of energies in concentration—bring forth possibilities of transformation and evolution from deep within the self.

A talisman serves as a physical representation of the changes we wish to call into our lives. Its visual elements are in harmony with our desired transformation. The word *talisman* comes from the ancient Greek word *telesma,* meaning "to complete or perform a rite." In Chapter 6, you will learn how to create your own ritual, or rite, to charge your talisman with the powers you desire to bring into your life.

This process does not omit the need for the deep work of unearthing your underlying patterns and habits, but it can assist with the integration and acceptance of these less desirable elements of self. It is wonderful to have intentions, but it's just as important to do the work of releasing yourself from your own unconscious patterns. Having a reminder of these intentions in the form of handcrafted art allows you to not only connect to your desire for evolution in the creation of your talisman but also have a frequent visual reminder in your day-to-day experience.

Creating a talisman through embroidery isn't just about making something that looks nice. The physical act of embroidering brings a thread from below to above and back again, traveling across realms in a meditative, repetitive act. This integration of above and below mirrors the way symbols bring messages from the conscious *above* world to the subconscious, underworld realms *below*.

The Science of Slowness

Embroidery is in its essence a slow process. Stitching cannot be rushed, designs are built in a gradual manner, and great joy can be found in this gentle evolution. This makes it the perfect craft for contemplation on how our lives can benefit from a slow buildup of design.

Until recent history, the slow growth reflected in the natural world and in the required crafts of daily living was all there was. Our bodies and minds evolved thanks to, and in support of, slow growth. Today, we live in a culture that not only makes it possible to force growth but often expects it. While we don't have to eschew technological or human progress, we must weave the appreciation for slow growth back into the tapestry of our lives if we hope to move toward a more harmonious relationship with the natural environment that surrounds us.

Embroidery offers an opportunity to return to the natural order. Stitching by hand slows down the body and, over time, slows down the mind. It brings us out of the expedited expectations of the

beta brain wave state (characteristic of a strongly engaged active mind) and into the calmer, more restful alpha brain wave state. While the beta state of heightened awareness is great for navigating heavy traffic or managing a daily schedule, it can also bring feelings of restlessness and unnecessary stress if we don't engage in activities to transition out of this state. Learning to move the brain into states of

The meditative process of embroidering can help bring the mind into a restful state of brain activity.

slower frequencies can make getting to sleep (delta state) much easier and deeper, which supports our ability to recover from stress in the long run.

There is mind-altering magic available through engaging in your own creative pursuits. Bringing yourself into the alpha state—a more relaxed state that enhances learning and intuition—helps you access the subconscious mind, which is where your beliefs in your own reality and abilities lie. This means that engaging in calming activities such as drawing, meditation, and handcrafting can not only calm the mind and bring your body to a state of balance but also help you confront and reprogram deep-seated beliefs so you can visualize new realities for yourself.

There is one prerequisite to using creative practices to access these lower brain wave states: Keep your expectations at bay. One of the most important lessons I teach in my workshops is that, contrary to what we have been taught, the lower your expectations are about the outcome of a creative practice, the more fulfilling and rewarding the practice of making art can be.

A NOTE ON DIVINITY

Throughout these pages you'll notice references to the energies of the cosmos, the universe, and divine forces. I'm not here to tell you whether there is or isn't a god; I have no religious motives, and I believe each individual should choose whatever works for them. That said, I do believe there is an underlying force in the universe that keeps the planets moving in orbit, keeps the flowers emerging from the ground each spring, and allows us to experience transcendent wonders such as dreams, love, death, and rainbows. You can call this God, the universe, gravity, or quantum physics—whatever you want to believe in. I'll call this underlying energy "divine" or "cosmic" for the sake of clarity and consistency. Feel free to translate this to reflect your own beliefs.

Transformative Qualities of the Creative Process

Creativity is a conversation and collaboration between a variety of sources—our personal intention, our current capabilities, and the divine essence of the materials we work with. By opening ourselves up to creative expansion, we can discover the path that brings us home to ourselves.

Putting too much emphasis on technique can leave us feeling inadequate, unskilled, or like we'll never be good enough. Let's shift our attention to meaning, to intention, and to the stories within us that we can express despite (or even in support of) our limited abilities. This is not a book that requires perfect stitching; in fact, you may notice that my stitches are frequently imperfect. These areas that might be considered sloppy by traditional needlework standards are the elements that remind me of the humanity and intention brought to these stitches.

Many years ago, an art teacher of mine told me, "The camera has already been invented." What she hinted to my young and tender ears was: It is not your job to replicate reality, it is your job to bring your own visions into reality. This was perhaps one of the most influential teachings of my entire life. While I did go on to learn exactly how to describe three-dimensional forms in paint and pencil, casting shadows and creating perspective, I found myself as an adult artist trying to unlearn all that formalism in order to access the reality in the depths of my psyche that wanted to be shown to the world—imperfections required.

Keep in mind as you work with this book that there is no one way to stitch. There is no one meaning behind a symbol. There is no one arrangement of symbols that works best. There is no best, there are only multitudes.

Tools for Accessing Creativity

The best tool for a new creative practice is a new mind-set, especially if you've been trained to experience life primarily through rational and literal methods. Research suggests that with regular practice, meditation and other forms of relaxation can improve our reactions to stress by reprogramming the brain's response, allowing us to approach stressful situations with a clearer and more focused mind.

On the following pages I describe a few practices I've found helpful to stimulate and enhance the creative process while releasing stress, anxiety, and attachment to expectations. They can change your vibrations, open you up to new possibilities, and require only your time, focus, and trust in your own ability to transform.

Vibrant Visualizations

Have you ever found yourself drifting so far into your imagination that you could swear you physically left the room you're sitting in? Maybe you were frequently reprimanded for daydreaming in school or at work? If this sounds like you, then you're in for a treat!

Vibrant visualization is something everyone does whether they know it or not. When your partner or roommate asks if you know where the lid to the blender is, you might visualize your kitchen cabinets and drawers. Or when you're walking or driving through town, you're visualizing the sidewalks or roads that will get you where you need to go.

How can this help with embroidery? When the rational, decision-making part of the brain learns to work in harmony with the intuitive, imaginative parts of the brain responsible for visualization (creating something that does not yet exist), you can more clearly make decisions on which colors to use, how large an embroidered shape should be, and where exactly it should be placed in the composition.

Beyond the physical realm of embroidery, being able to visualize is a key skill in personal transformation. We have the ability to enact change in our own lives—with our intentions, with our words, and with the spaces we create for ourselves. Allowing ourselves time in the imaginal realms is what empowers us and reminds us of our ability to evolve and to create things for ourselves.

Clear Light Meditation

Conjuring up a clear sparkling light of purification within your mind may seem like an *out-there* practice, but when you allow yourself to feel radiant from within, it can really transform your mood. Begin with a few deep, grounding breaths to calm your system. When you feel focused and present, imagine a tiny globe of glowing light at the core of your chest, just underneath the center of your sternum.

On your next inhalation, breathe into this globe of light and feel it expand a bit. Continue breathing deeply, and feel this globe of light expanding with each inhale until you find yourself surrounded by glowing light. If you'd like to keep going, imagine this light filling up your home, expanding out to your neighborhood, lighting up your entire town with radiant beams of light. When you're finished, allow the globe of light to gently return to its original size, taking a few deep breaths in the darkness of your closed eyes.

You can also try this visualization using colored lights, such as lavender, blue, or gold (see Color Harmony on page 108 for more on the influence of color), or even sparkling glitter. This is a space for you to get creative and use your imagination!

Heaven and Earth Meditation

This meditation brings us back to our role as an active participant in the natural world by stepping into the connection between the earth below us and the cosmos above.

Begin in a comfortable seated position, in a chair, cross-legged, whatever works as long as your spine remains straight and tall. Imagine a cord tied to the crown of your head that is being pulled upward, lengthening your spine while you remain grounded in your seat.

Begin to visualize roots growing out of the base of your spine, reaching down through the floor into the ground below you, deep into the earth. After growing these roots, on your next inhale, breathe in the nurturing energies of the soil through your roots, and as you exhale allow these energies to fill the space of your entire body. Feel this rising and filling of earth's energies for a few breaths before calling on the cosmos.

When you feel rooted, visualize the vastness of the cosmos past the skies above you. Now, on an inhale, imagine the crown of your head opening up and absorbing this cosmic energy, this divine order that keeps our galaxy spinning in perfect harmony. Allow this cosmic light to fill your body. And as you

exhale, release this energy down into the earth through your newly formed roots. Exchange the energies of the nourishing earth below and the spacious harmonies above, sending them through you as you breathe.

When you feel sufficiently connected, pull your roots back up into your body and take a few grounding breaths before gently opening your eyes.

Reconnect with Your Magic Hands

One of our greatest superpowers is one we regularly take for granted. Our hands are a source of potent magic in the most basic sense through their abilities to transform and manipulate objects in the world, and in the most advanced sense by healing through the laying-on of hands.

Our hands are conduits for energy, our own personal satellites sending and receiving energetic waves. We can use them to channel energy outward to a person or object, and we can also use them to absorb energy from another person or object. From a purely scientific perspective, our fingers are a primary source for gaining tactile information, as they contain a dense collection of nerve endings. Consider the number of unconscious messages being sent from the hands to the brain and back again during the action of our days.

Most of the time, we do not acknowledge the power our hands possess and we don't recognize their possibilities. When we take a moment to reconnect to our hands, to recognize and show gratitude to the dexterity available to us (thanks to a most beneficial evolution), we can infuse all that we make and touch with a personal intention. Through recognition of the powers in our hands, we can go beyond stitching as a visually transformative process to an energetically transformative process.

1. Let your eyes rest closed while you take a few deep breaths and rub your hands together until they produce a bit of heat.

2. Open your eyes slowly while gently pulling your hands apart just a bit, feeling the energy created as it bounces back and forth between your palms.

3. Cup both hands as if you're cradling a ball and take a few moments to look at them. Admire their lines, their muscles, appreciating scars as well as beauty.

4. Turn both palms up toward the sky, even if you are indoors, and feel them absorbing the light from the sun. Feel this bright light flow through your arms and down into your body. (In winter, actually going outside and absorbing the sun's energies on your bare palms can do wonders for raising your mood.)

5. Now, place both palms on the ground and envision pumping energy down through your arms and out your hands back into the earth.

6. To end, clap your hands together in celebration of their strength!

Box Breathing

This technique equalizes the breath to calm the nervous system. It can be used in high-stress conditions to return the body to homeostasis after the fight-or-flight response kicks in.

Spend a few seconds in each stage of breath: inhale, hold breath in; exhale, hold breath out. The time spent in each stage depends on what is comfortable for you. You may start with three or four seconds in each stage, and move up to longer if it is more calming. So, box breathing goes:

1. Inhale for four seconds.

2. Hold breath in for four seconds.

3. Exhale for four seconds.

4. Hold breath out for four seconds.

You can visualize each stage as an equal side of a box. Repeat this sequence for several minutes to encourage the mind to enter a more focused and calm state.

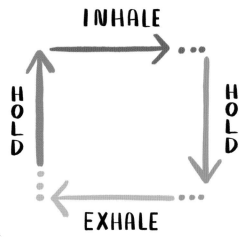

Dance with Your Eyes Closed

This one's easy—no fancy techniques or descriptions, just put on some music, clear the floor, close your eyes, and *dance!* I'd say about 95 percent of my visual inspiration comes from this activity.

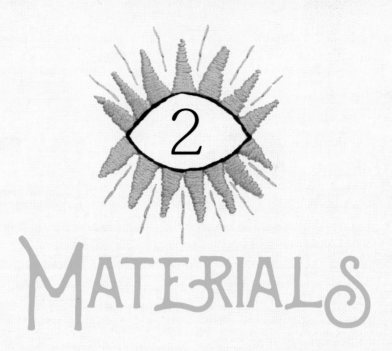

MATERIALS

Part of the beauty of embroidery lies in simple materials. You don't need to invest much to begin. Working with garments you own or salvaging old linens makes for ecologically and financially sound stitching experiments. Start with the basics: quality fabric and classic embroidery floss. Although, embroidery can be done on a wide range of materials; some of my early work was made by stitching on wooden panels. The best way to know if a material works for embroidery is to give it a try.

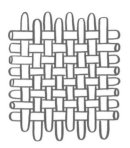

Woven fabric

Knit fabric is trickier to work with than woven fabric.

Fabric

As the canvas for your work of art, fabric is equally as important as the designs you create. After spending many hours on my first large-scale embroidery, I learned an important lesson the hard way—cheap fabrics are not improved by elaborate stitches! Stick with high-quality natural fibers for your designs. Choose a woven fabric thick enough that you cannot see through it easily but woven loose enough to pass a needle through without forcing it. Some of my favorite fabrics for embroidery are muslin, denim, raw silk, broadcloth, chambray, and anything labeled as "shirting." These sturdy wovens can hold the tension of the threads without getting bunched. Lightweight fabrics or knit fabrics are not recommended for beginners (though you can try a thicker knit that is not stretchy). The best test for embroidery fabric is to try it out! So test a few stitches someplace.

Needles

The needle should have a large enough eye for embroidery thread to pass through easily. Don't try to use regular sewing needles. The opening in the eye should be as wide as the thread. Needles labeled as embroidery needles or crewel needles are good for most fabrics; they have a large eye and a sharp point that can easily pass through fine to medium fibers. Tapestry needles are used for embroidery on thick fabrics; with a large eye and a blunt point, they are able to pass through thicker fibers without snagging.

If the needle seems to be catching on the fibers of the fabric or causing snags, try a more blunt option. If the needle is having trouble passing through the fabric because it can't get through the weave, try a sharper needle. If you're having trouble getting the eye of the needle through the fabric, it's usually because of the friction of the thread on the fabric. In this case, use a needle with a larger eye so the thread can pass through easily.

Thread

One wonderful thing about embroidery is that you can use nearly anything you can thread a needle with to create designs. But there are three options traditionally used: perle cotton, embroidery floss, and sashiko threads. Perle threads have a rope-like texture; they cannot be split, but they come in many sizes. Embroidery floss and sashiko threads come in one size, and the single strand of floss is made up of six strands that can be split into two, three, or up to six individual strands. So you have six size options in one convenient package. You can, for instance, create a more delicate line by using only three of the six threads.

Splitting Your Thread

1. Cut thread to about 1 yard (36 inches).

2. At one end, separate the amount you want. I usually split the thread down to two or three strands, so I'm able to easily use the remaining quantity.

3. Grasp the two separated parts at the top ends and run your finger down the length of the thread and allow it to untwist freely at the bottom end. When you reach the bottom, separate the two sections and allow them to wind themselves back up. Be careful

they don't tangle back up with each other; threads tend to want to retwist immediately after separating!

4. Be sure to "love" your threads after splitting them (see below).

Embroidery thread is made up of six strands plied together, which you can easily pull apart for varying effects.

"LOVING" YOUR THREADS

When I studied fashion in college, I had the pleasure of working under designer Natalie Chanin, a master of slow fashion and a skilled embroiderer. Natalie's most basic teaching ended up being her most profound—the act of "loving" your threads for both physical and energetic assistance.

It's really quite simple: By stroking the length of the thread through the pressed tips of your fingers a few times before sewing, you're preparing the thread and ensuring fewer tangles. This removes any kinks or twists and allows you to infuse the thread with your energy and intentions. It also allows a tiny trace of body oil from your hands to lubricate the thread for better passage through the fabric.

Stick 1:
154
550
553
554
341
340
32
333
718
918
919
720
946
947
741
972
444
726

Stick 2:
221
3722
244
950
948
3864
3064
3772
356
758
3771
3770
712
829
3045
3046
612
610
3031
3862
3864
3033

Stick 3:
3826
977
976
975
301
780
869
680
3852
728
677
834
832
830
839
3371
3799
645
646
647
648
453
451
779

Stick 4:
504
502
520
934
3362
3363
3364
522
3819
733
730
469
3347
470
581
166
3013
3012
3011

Stick 5:
3817
562
3815
561
500
823
3750
791
798
931
3752
3753

DMC uses number codes for their colors. Here are the colors used in this book for quick reference.

CREATING YOUR COLOR PALETTE

If you havent noticed already, embroidery threads come in hundreds of colors. My go-to brand, DMC, carries 500 shades! This is equal parts amazing and totally overwhelming, which is why I try to keep my palette narrowed down to 70 to 80 colors. This means when I go looking for a yellow I don't have to sort through dozens of yellows but can choose from about 10 options that I know look good with the other colors I use frequently.

Creating your own palette will take time, but it's well worth the effort when you know you can place an order for your favorite colors and not be surprised at what you get. Look at the colors you choose most often for home décor and clothing. This is a great place to get an idea of the colors you'll likely use most in embroidery. After this "personal favorites" color research, start your palette by choosing your favorite colors in person at your local craft store. While it's great to have hundreds of options available online, seeing the colors in real life and knowing these colors are stocked locally is even better!

Helpful Hints

※ One cool thing about sashiko and perle threads is that after removing them from the packaging, you end up with one big loop. If you cut this loop open, you get a bunch of embroidery floss at the exact length needed to sew with (about 1 yard), and it saves you time trying to untangle threads. I usually tie a rubber band around one end of this pile to keep the lengths together, or loop them onto a metal ring and store them hanging.

※ Most brands of embroidery floss, like DMC, can be kept in their wrappers and the threads can be pulled from the barcode end. Hold on to the wrapper, find the loose end at the bottom of the skein, and pull it gently.

※ You can also use wool or another yarn, though it's best to follow the general rule of thumb: Thicker yarns work best on thicker, sturdier fabrics, and thinner yarns look best with thinner, smooth fabrics.

Setting Up Your Hoop

For some mysterious reason, I spent years avoiding the hoop. I was convinced it was cumbersome and unnecessary. I was so wrong! This convenient and affordable tool makes it easy to transfer patterns, and prevents you from creating too-tight stitches that cause puckering in the finished work of art.

The traditional style of embroidery hoop is composed of two parts: the outer hoop, which has a small screw, and the inner hoop, which is a continuous piece. The screw on the outer hoop is used for adjusting the tightness; do not unscrew it all the way, as it can sometimes be difficult to get the screw back in once removed. I use wood or bamboo hoops. There are two ways to set up your hoop. One is for use with tracing patterns so that the fabric lies flat against a hard surface. The other is for embroidery, with the fabric framed facing you.

✴ To prepare fabric for tracing a pattern, place the small continuous hoop on top of the fabric and tuck it into the adjustable hoop beneath the fabric. This keeps your fabric flush with the surface of your image to be transferred.

✴ To use a hoop for embroidery, place the continuous hoop underneath the fabric. Put the adjustable hoop on top and secure the fabric.

For both setups, start with the adjustable hoop a little loose while you center the fabric. Once you've got your fabric sandwiched in between the two hoops, tighten the adjustable hoop just enough so you can slide the fabric into the perfect position, but not so tight that you're distorting the weave of the fabric when you pull (this can damage the fabric). Now gently pull at the edges to make the fabric taut like a drumhead. Make sure the weave isn't distorted. You should be able to see the grid of the weave running straight up and down and straight back and forth like graph paper. When it's all set up, tighten the hoop one last time.

Be sure the fabric on your hoop is pulled taut, but not so tight that it distorts the weave.

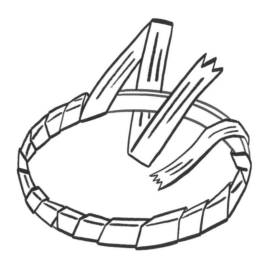

❋ Having trouble with your fabric coming loose? Try wrapping the continuous hoop with some cotton ribbon or a long strip of cotton fabric. Wrap it at a diagonal all the way around the hoop. This gives the hoop more texture and helps hold the fabric securely between the two hoops, instead of it slipping off the smooth wooden surface.

❋ Hard edges getting you down? Many hoops are a little sharp on the edge, which can cause permanent marking, especially on thinner or more delicate fibers. Using sandpaper, soften the outer edges of the continuous hoop to remove this sharp edge.

❋ Working with thicker fabrics? Thanks to the sturdy nature of thicker fibers, you won't need an embroidery hoop. Actually, many thicker fabrics won't even fit in the hoop if you try!

Marking Tools

For pattern transfers, work with a marking tool that will disappear. Even a #2 pencil—seemingly innocent and normally able to wash out—can leave marks behind that will drive you crazy for years. Take it from someone who has experienced this!

I love Caran d'Ache watercolor pencils in white or ivory because they are not waxy like Prismacolor or other colored pencils, and can be washed out. Do not use a darker color in these pencils because they could bleed and not wash out.

Crayola Ultra Clean Washable Markers come in many colors, and I have never had a problem with them leaving a permanent mark, though I recommend testing any markers or pencils before tracing.

Pilot FriXion pens are heat erasable, so the ink can be removed with a hair dryer or by gently ironing the back of the embroidery (not too hard—you don't want to smash your stitches).

There are other brands of washable and air-erase markers that are designed to wash out or fade over time. They are fine for most applications, though I find they can sometimes air-erase before I'm done stitching; in humid areas this can happen in just a few hours. They also do not seem to wash out of naturally dyed fabrics, and since that is a big chunk of the materials I use, I can't use them all the time. You've been warned!

Transfer Paper

Saral transfer paper comes in an affordable sampler pack of five colors, washes out, transfers nicely onto fabric, is reusable, and can be purchased from many different types of stores. Win, win, win, win, win!

There are also a variety of embroidery transfer papers that can go through the printer, then iron or stick onto the fabric. These are a great option if you do not feel confident in your tracing skills. Sulky and Pellon are two brands that offer a variety of these papers. I also love Printworks Vanishing Fabric Transfers and DMC Magic Paper.

Tracing Methods

There are myriad methods and tools available to trace embroidery designs onto fabric. I find the light-box method to be most convenient and effective. If the fabric is darker or thicker, you may want to use the transfer paper method.

Before you trace your design, you'll need to find the center of both the fabric and the printed pattern. Simply fold each of them in half in both directions. The point where the folds meet is the center. Line up this point on the fabric and the pattern together.

Fold your pattern in half in both directions. Then fold your fabric in half in both directions. Line up the two center points.

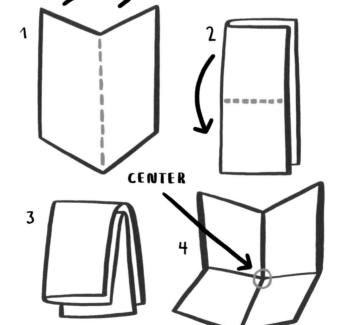

CENTER

Light-Box Method

You can use an actual light box, a window on a bright day, or even a glass table with a flashlight underneath it.

꙰ Start by taping the paper pattern onto the glass. Then, place the fabric faceup over the paper. Be sure to center the fabric properly. Keep the fabric in the same place; tape the fabric down on four sides if needed.

꙰ With the light coming through the back of the glass, you should be able to see the pattern through the fabric. Carefully trace the pattern onto the fabric with your marking tool of choice. Be careful to not tear the paper—or break the glass!

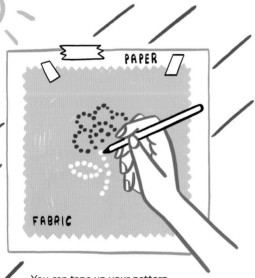

You can tape up your pattern onto a window to trace it onto fabric. Be careful not to press too hard on the glass.

Transfer Paper Method

The transfer paper method is a good option if you are using fabric that is too dark or thick to work with a light box. You can buy pattern transfer paper from a fabric store or make your own using chalk. I have not had luck with graphite transfer paper (sold at art stores) unless the fabric is incredibly smooth and thin. Pattern transfer paper (sold at fabric stores) is designed for use on almost all fabrics; it is washable and comes in a variety of colors. To make your own transfer paper, simply rub white chalk all over the back of the pattern you wish to transfer, then give the pattern paper a little shake to get rid of any excess chalk.

꙰ You'll need a hard, smooth surface to get a sharp line, so place the fabric faceup on a table.

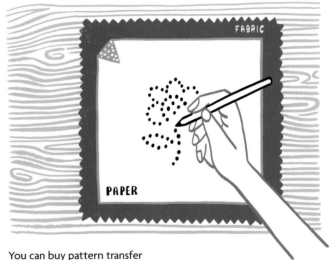

You can buy pattern transfer paper or make your own with white chalk. You'll have to press hard with an instrument to get the chalk onto the fabric, and then go over the chalk lines with a marking tool as well.

* Place the paper pattern on the fabric chalk-side down, centering it as desired.

* Use a dull-tip pencil or the back end of a small paintbrush to trace the design. Be careful not to tear the paper. Keep the paper in the same spot; you can tape it onto the fabric if you're worried about it sliding around.

* Pull up the paper pattern and use a white pencil or washable marker to go over the lines again. The chalk will fade quickly, so use a marking tool to keep the lines visible for the entirety of your embroidery project.

Perforation Method

Another popular method is to use a piece of paper with the design drawn on it, and poke holes along the lines of the design every ¼ to ½ inch. Then, mark the fabric through these holes. Yes, this is as time consuming as it sounds, which is why I much prefer the light-box or transfer paper method.

Getting Started with Thread

I've watched so many beginners and even skilled stitchers wrestling with long lengths of thread in an attempt to avoid having to thread a needle more frequently. The irony is, in the time you'll spend managing tangles and pulling these long lengths through the fabric, you could have threaded the needle dozens of times.

The outstretched arm reaches about 36 inches (1 yard) from the fabric, so I suggest starting with a thread this length. This allows you to pull the thread all the way through the fabric in one quick motion.

Knotting the Thread

To knot the end of the thread, I use one square knot on top of another. This knot is usually large enough to keep the thread secure on the fabric. If your knots are slipping through or if you're working with a thinner fabric and the knots seem too bulky, you can create a knot on the fabric by using the knot-on-fabric technique, detailed on the facing page. These will eventually be covered by the remaining stitches in your embroidery.

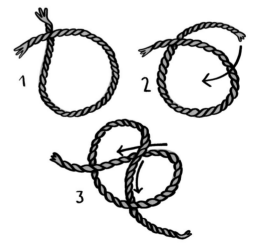

Knot-on-Fabric

If you're working with delicate or loosely woven fabric, you may find the knot pulling through from the back. If this happens, try this knot-on-fabric technique: Bring the needle through the fabric from the back to the front, leaving a 2-inch tail on the back. While holding this tail on the back, create two or three very tiny (⅛ inch or smaller) stitches on top of one another in a little X. Be sure to do this in an area that will be covered by the finished embroidery stitches so it'll be well hidden. Because different fabrics and threads react differently, you can test if your knot is strong enough by letting go of the tail and tugging at the long thread at the front. If the threads don't pull through, you're good to stitch! If the stitches come loose, try again with an extra stitch on top of your X.

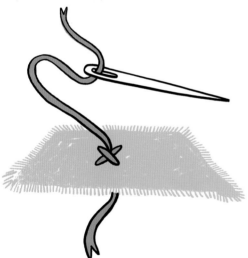

Threading the Needle

You've got a needle with a large eye, and your embroidery floss has been "loved" and knotted. Now it's time to get this baby threaded. Threading the needle is easiest when you've cut the thread cleanly with *sharp* scissors. Moistening the end of the thread can help immensely (I won't judge you if you do this with your tongue).

This is the method that has worked well for me:

✳ Pinch the freshly cut end of the thread between your thumb and forefinger and place the eye of the needle over where the end will come out between your fingertips.

✳ As you slowly roll the tips of your fingers outward to expose the end of the thread, push the needle down into this end, giving the thread nowhere to go but into the eye of the needle.

If threading the needle takes you a ridiculous amount of time, invest a few dollars in a needle threader, or upgrade to a larger-eye needle. The needle threaders that last the longest are a single piece of metal with a hook on one end. LoRan makes a great affordable one. If you can't pull the thread through with one of these, you probably need a needle with a bigger eye.

3

STITCH METHODS

Countless stitches have been developed since the needle was invented 45,000 years ago (give or take a few). Some have stuck around longer than others. These foundational stitches provide you with a beautiful range of textures and weights to play with in your designs. They can also be easily transformed by switching up the length, width, or thread weight they are stitched with. Get creative with these and try your own variations of them.

A sampler is the classic teaching tool to test out new stitches in a neat and orderly way. I wanted to give the sampler a bit of an upgrade and turn it into a work of art I'd be proud to put on display.

Up through fabric

Down in designated spot

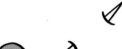

Push all the way through fabric

Anatomy of a Stitch Illustration

All embroidery begins with the needle and thread under the fabric. You've threaded the needle and knotted the thread. Now pull from the back of the fabric to the front so the knot is on the back. This point where the thread is first brought to the front of the fabric is shown in the top illustration at left. The next two points are made in one motion before pulling the thread all the way through (see below about the traditional vs. quick methods of stitching). Typically, stitch illustrations show these three motions all together in one sketch, but I've shown each step separately so they are easier to read for beginners.

Stitch illustrations usually show a short amount of thread, but you'll likely have a much longer piece to manage (though no more than 1 yard, I hope). Pay attention in the illustrations to the end that is coming out of the fabric vs. the end that is threaded through the needle (the end coming out of the needle is illustrated with a scruffy frayed edge).

Traditional vs. Quick Methods of Stitching

Most traditional needleworkers will say you need to insert the needle straight down into the fabric and pull all the way to the back before piercing the fabric again and pulling it all the way up to the front. For example, in the illustration below showing the traditional method, step 2 would be one motion and step 3 would be another motion. This makes sense if you have an embroidery hoop in a hoop stand and both hands are free, but if you're holding the hoop with your hand it can get a little cumbersome. So I do actions 2 and 3 before pulling the thread through.

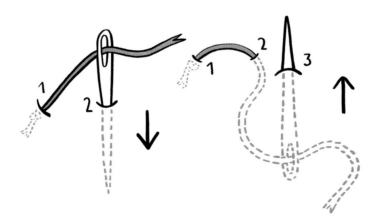

Come up through the fabric (step 1), then back down (step 2). Pull all the way to the back of the fabric. Then push back up to the front of the fabric (step 3). The dotted lines in the illustration show the needle and thread under the fabric.

This is not a guide to traditional needlework, and I honestly have never noticed a difference except that the traditional way takes longer! Some people prefer to do certain stitches this way for the sake of precision, and that is up to you. Some stitches, like the split stitch, can only be done the traditional way, but here you have a choice. Try both ways and see what you like!

Beginning Your Stitches

All the stitches in this chapter begin in the same way—by knotting the thread and pulling the thread through from back to front so the knot on the back of the fabric holds the thread securely. Bring the tip of the needle up at the beginning of your line of stitching.

TIPS AS YOU BEGIN

✳ Try to keep your stitches a little loose. If your fabric is puckering or seems ripply, your stitches are too tight. You don't need to pull until the thread is tight—just pull until the thread lies flat on the fabric. A little slack is fine and will ensure the final piece of work doesn't warp the fabric and create wrinkles. Also, cotton threads often shrink a tiny bit in the wash. If you're embroidering on clothing that will end up being laundered, be sure to leave a little slack in your stitches. I've never in all my workshops seen a student create stitches that were too loose. Our tendency seems to be more toward creating stitches that are too tight—so loosen up a little, would ya?

✳ When working on curved lines you may have to use a smaller stitch, so keep this in mind when planning your design. Imagine connecting dots to create a line. If you have a sharp curve, a long stitch will make it look more like a corner, while a bunch of tiny stitches gives a more fluid effect.

✳ Get experimental. Some of the most exciting effects are made not by re-creating the stitches exactly as described but by pushing the possibilities and exploring how many different ways they can be created. Try making the stitches irregular or elongating certain elements. Try them out in different yarns, ribbons, or even wire.

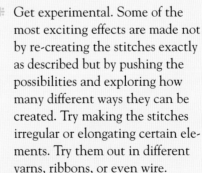

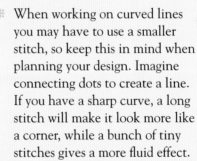

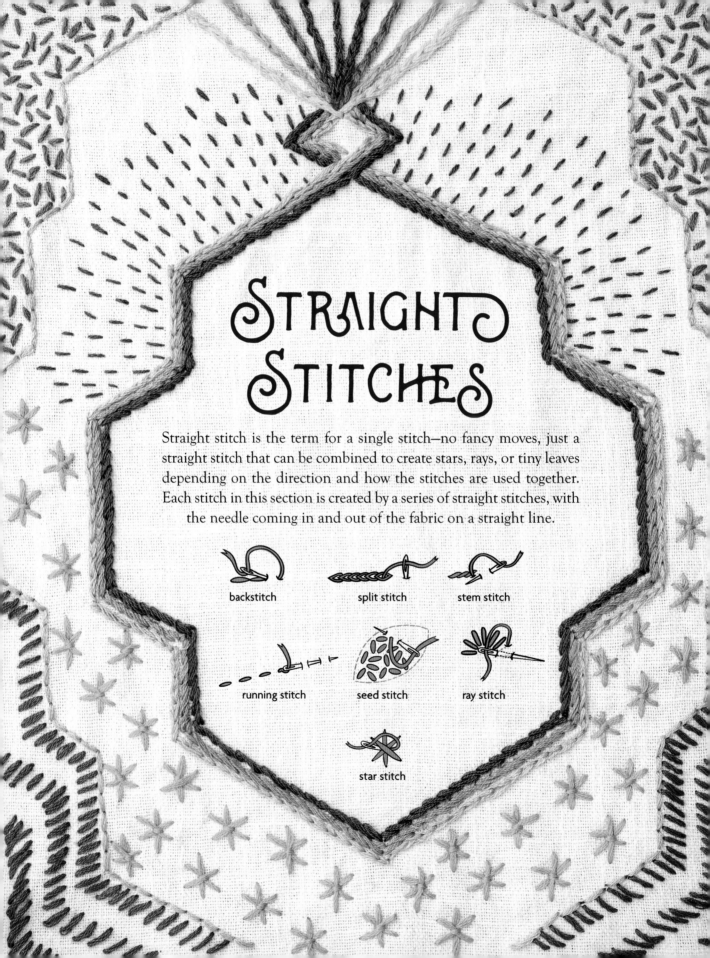

STRAIGHT STITCHES

Straight stitch is the term for a single stitch—no fancy moves, just a straight stitch that can be combined to create stars, rays, or tiny leaves depending on the direction and how the stitches are used together. Each stitch in this section is created by a series of straight stitches, with the needle coming in and out of the fabric on a straight line.

backstitch

split stitch

stem stitch

running stitch

seed stitch

ray stitch

star stitch

Backstitch

This classic continuous stitch is used for outlines and fine details, and closely resembles a sewing machine stitch. For fine detail work, use shorter-length stitches of ⅛ inch and split the embroidery floss down to two or three strands.

1. After bringing the needle up at the beginning of the line, insert the needle back into the fabric a little less than ¼ inch (or whatever stitch length you've chosen) from where the thread came out.

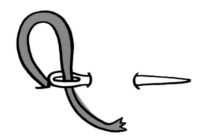

2. Bring the needle back out this same distance ahead, and pull the thread through until taut.

3. Insert the needle back into the closest end of this first stitch.

4. Bring the needle out one stitch length ahead of where the thread just came out.

5. Continue inserting the needle into the end of the previous stitch.

6. Continue exiting one stitch length ahead to create a solid, continuous line.

Split Stitch

This smooth and fluid line is created by "splitting" the previous stitch. As with the backstitch, be sure to make shorter stitches when creating tight curves with the split stitch.

1. Bring the needle up at the beginning of the line. Insert the needle into the fabric one stitch length ahead (about ¼ inch, or shorter for details and curved lines).

2. Pull the thread through all the way to the back until the stitch lies flat.

3. Bring the needle up in the middle of this first stitch, piercing through and "splitting" the thread.

4. Insert the needle back into the fabric ¼ inch from this point and pull to the back.

5. Repeat, each time splitting up through the previous stitch.

Stem Stitch

To create this ropelike effect, you'll be making stitches slightly offset from one another. For tight curves and details, keep this stitch very short, ⅛ inch or so.

1. After bringing the needle out of the fabric at the beginning of the line of stitching, insert the needle about ¼ to ⅜ inch along the line. The dots in the illustration indicate where the needle will come in and out of the fabric. It may also help to learn this stitch by marking the fabric with dots spaced ¼ inch apart.

2. With the needle facing the direction you started, bring the needle back out at the halfway mark between where the thread came out and where the needle went in.

3. Now insert the needle one stitch length ahead; the end of the previous stitch will line up with the middle of this new stitch.

4. Bring the needle out at the end of the last stitch.

5. Continue along the stitch line marked, being sure each stitch is the same length.

 TIP Be sure that the needle is coming out of the same side on every stitch for a consistent look. As you work, the tip of the needle should be facing your previous stitches.

THE S AND Z RULE
When creating a piece of work with multiple stem stitches, it will look best if the stitches are going at the same angle. The best way to remember this is the S and Z rule: Is the angle of your previous stitches creating the angle of the letter S or the letter Z?

Running Stitch

Created by a simple running in and out of the fabric with the needle, this stitch can be made in a variety of ways for different results. You can create an even stitch length so the part of the thread that goes under the fabric is the same length as the part that is seen above. Or you can choose to make longer stitches on top, only picking up a tiny bit of fabric between stitches. Or you can create tiny stitches on the top of the fabric while the needle goes behind the fabric for larger gaps in between stitches.

1. Bring the thread to the surface. Insert the needle back into the fabric at the desired distance of the stitches on the surface.

2. Bring the needle back out along the stitch line.

3. Continue this in and out motion; once you get the hang of it, you can even create multiple running stitches in the same motion before pulling the thread through.

TIP When making curved lines with the running stitch, you may need to use smaller stitches and pick up fewer stitches at a time. Keeping the running stitches under ⅜ inch prevents snagging on wearable items.

Seed Stitch

This texture is created by making random running stitches and is usually used to fill in areas. There are many options for this technique. You can stitch them close together for an opaque effect. You can overlap the stitches for full coverage. Or you can vary the distance or size of the stitch to create shading. This method works best when the chaos of stitches on the back is hidden, so use an opaque fabric. This is one of those challenges where you're required to be consistently inconsistent. It may take some practice to get the hang of it. Think of it like sprinkles on a cupcake, or pickup sticks. They all scatter about in different directions, creating an exciting pattern of chaos.

Ray Stitch

The ray stitch is another type of running stitch. To create expanding rays, bring the needle to the surface at the top of the first ray, then back into the fabric at the bottom of the ray. Running the needle under the fabric diagonally, bring it out again at the top of the second ray and then back at the bottom of that ray. Continue until the last ray is complete.

Star Stitch

This is a simple way to create celestial stars composed of three straight stitches overlapping and one stitch holding them down in the middle. The order of the three stitches that make the star is not important, but it can help to mark them out first so the spacing is right.

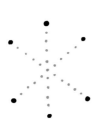

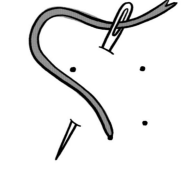

1. Start by marking six dots for the points of your star. It helps to visualize how they will connect, but you don't need to draw the dotted lines connecting the points.

2. Bring the thread up at one end of a ray. Insert the tip of the needle into the point on the opposite side. You can pull the thread to the back and come up at the next point, or you can take a shortcut by inserting the tip of the needle in the next point before pulling through the thread. This will bring you back on top and ready to stitch the next ray.

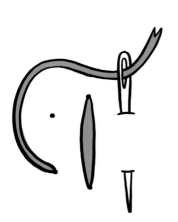

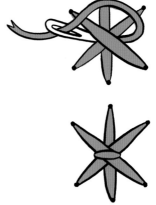

3–4. Repeat step 2 with the remaining rays, overlapping them in the middle.

5. Bring the tip of the needle up at one side of the overlapped center. Tack down these three stitches by inserting the needle into the other side of the inter-section, and pull the thread flat.

TUCK STITCHES

Tuck stitches are a bit more complex and require a second step before pulling the needle through. After inserting the needle in and out of the fabric, the thread should be tucked behind the tip of the needle before pulling it all the way through. This also means each stitch is being held by the stitch created after it. So the final stitch must always be tacked down with a small stitch on the other side of the last tuck.

chain stitch

wrapped chain stitch

detached chain stitch

fly stitch

feather stitch

blanket stitch

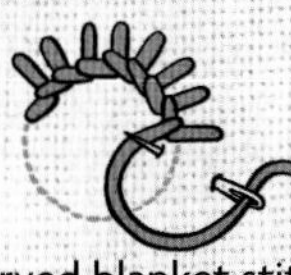

curved blanket stitch

Chain Stitch

For the chain stitch, you'll insert the needle back into the same spot the thread came out of. This can feel unnatural after learning the previous stitches, but you'll love it once you get the hang of it!

 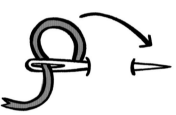

TUCK BEHIND NEEDLE

1. Bring the needle out at the end of the stitch line, then insert the needle into the fabric at this same point, but don't pull through yet!

2. Position the tip of the needle to come out ¼ inch away from where it went in.

3. At this point, when you've got the needle coming out of the fabric, before you pull it through, tuck the thread behind the needle so that the next stitch catches this stitch.

4. Pull the needle through until the loop is gently secured against where the thread comes out, but not so tight that the loop pulls on the loose thread. Now insert the needle back inside this loop, right where the thread just came out.

5. Bring the tip of the needle out ¼ inch down the stitch line, but don't pull through yet.

6. Tuck the thread behind the needle, then pull through until the stitch creates a gentle loop nestled into the previous loop.

TIP If you do not catch the thread behind the needle on each stitch, it will not create the stitch and you are left with a loose loop that can quickly unravel.

PULL TO BACK ↓

TO END

7. To end the chain stitch, insert the needle into the fabric on the outside of this loop to tack down this last stitch and prevent all the stitches from coming undone. This can be done with a tiny stitch to create a blunt end, or a long stitch to taper the end of the chain stitch.

Points and Turns with Chain Stitch

When turning corners with a chain stitch, it's best to end the stitch and begin a new chain stitch at the corner, slightly overlapping the end stitch so there is no gap in the line where the new stitch begins (A).

To create tapered points with a chain stitch, stagger the threads at the beginning of the stitch so the loop is a little narrower (B). Then continue normally. To end the stitch with a taper, create an elongated end stitch ¼ to ½ inch depending on how tapered you want the end (C). On sharp corners where two lines meet, slightly stagger the ends so that one line is shorter to create a more gentle tapered effect (D).

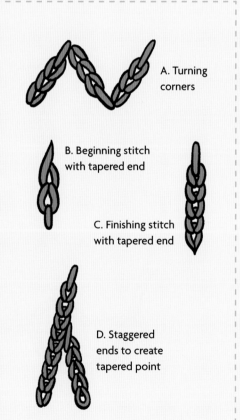

A. Turning corners

B. Beginning stitch with tapered end

C. Finishing stitch with tapered end

D. Staggered ends to create tapered point

Wrapped Chain Stitch

After creating a chain stitch, using a new thread, bring the needle up at the end of the chain stitch on the right side. Insert the needle underneath the chain stitch from the right to the left. Do not insert the needle through the fabric. Pull until it gently wraps over the stitch. Repeat this wrapping motion to create a ropelike effect, never inserting the needle into the fabric but just wrapping it over and under the chain stitch. When finished, insert the needle back into the fabric on the right side and tie it at the back.

Detached Chain Stitch

Often called the daisy stitch, a detached chain stitch is created with the first and last step of the chain stitch, securing the end of a single loop. When stitched around a circle, you can make sweet flowers.

1. Like with the chain stitch, bring the needle out at the end of the stitch line, then insert the needle into the fabric at this same point.

2. Position the tip of the needle to come out ¼ inch away from where it went in, and before you pull through, tuck the thread behind the needle.

3. Pull the needle through until the loop lies snug against the thread coming out of the middle, then tack down this stitch by inserting the needle into the outside of the loop.

Fly Stitch

The fly stitch creates little arrows that can be used in a variety of ways. With the corner pointing up, they can be tiny trees or mountains. With the corner pointing down, they become birds on a horizon.

1. Instead of inserting the needle in the same spot the thread came out (like the chain stitch), you'll insert the needle about ¼ inch to the side of where the thread came out.

2. Bring the tip of the needle out about ¼ inch above and in the middle between these two points.

3. Before pulling the needle through, tuck the thread behind the needle.

4. Tack this stitch down by inserting the needle above this point (on the other side of the V shape made by the thread), creating a small stitch. Pull through to the back to secure.

Fly Stitch Variation

The fly stitch can be used in multiples to create an arrow pattern by elongating the end stitch.

1. Follow steps 1 through 3 of the fly stitch instructions. Instead of tacking down this shape with a small stitch, insert the needle ¼ inch above the fly stitch and bring the tip of the needle out to the side at one end of the next fly stitch.

2. Insert the needle into the fabric on the other side. Bring it out at the end of the last tacked stitch and tuck the thread behind the needle tip before pulling through.

3. Continue to tack down the previous fly stitch with long stitches of equal length.

Feather Stitch

This uses the "tuck" method of the chain and fly stitches to create a continuous pattern of connected fly stitches. You can go back in and add more feather stitches onto the first one, slipping the needle under the ends to simulate the tuck stitch when connecting with the previous line of feather stitch.

1. After bringing the thread out at the top of the design, insert the needle about ¼ inch to the right of where the thread came out, similar to the fly stitch.

2. Bring the tip of the needle out about ¼ inch below and in the middle between these two points, and tuck the thread behind the tip of the needle before pulling through.

3. Insert the needle about ¼ inch to the right of where the thread came out.

4. Bring the tip out about ¼ inch below and in the middle between these two points, tucking the thread behind the needle before pulling through.

5. Insert the needle ¼ inch to the left of where the thread came out, bringing the tip of the needle out ¼ inch below and to the middle, and tucking the thread before pulling through. Repeat from left to right. For a wide feather stitch, make three stitches to the right, then three stitches to the left.

Blanket Stitch

The blanket stitch is used decoratively, for finishing edges, or to finish patches of fabric. Like the chain stitch, each stitch is held down by the stitch that comes after it, so be sure to tuck your thread behind the needle each time before pulling through. This stitch looks like little stems coming off a straight line of stitches, but each stem is actually part of the straight line.

1. After bringing the needle out to begin, insert the tip about ¼ inch away from and ¼ inch above where the thread came out.

2. Bring the tip of the needle out on the same line where the last stitch came out (the needle should be perpendicular to the line), tucking the thread behind the tip of the needle before pulling through.

3. Continue, inserting the needle about ¼ inch away from and ¼ inch above where the thread came out. If it helps, imagine this stitch as a series of squares in a row.

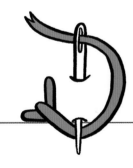

4. The needle should be inserted at a right angle to the direction of the line of stitching, catching the thread behind the needle for each stitch.

5. To finish, secure the final stitch with a tiny tack by inserting the needle on the other side of the loop.

Curved Blanket Stitch

Using the same tuck technique but on a curved line or in a circle, this blanket stitch can be done with the spokes fanning outward or with the spokes heading inward. It helps to draw both arc shapes, the inner and the outer edge of the flower or wheel, before stitching.

FLOWER MOTIF

  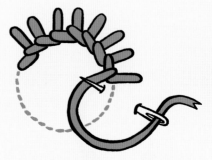

1. Begin with the thread coming out of the inner circle. Insert the needle into the outer edge of the circle and bring it out at the inner edge a tiny bit away from where the thread came out. Tuck the thread behind the tip of the needle before pulling through.

2. Repeat with wider spacing between stitches on the outer curved line, and barely any spacing on the inner curved line.

3. Continue on around the curved lines. End with a tiny tack to secure the last stitch, which should connect the last stitch to the beginning of the first stitch.

WHEEL MOTIF

The wheel motif, like the flower motif in reverse, works best if stitches are fairly close together, no more than ¼ inch apart.

   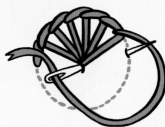

1. Begin with the thread coming out of the outer edge. Insert the needle into the inner edge.

2. Aim the point back through the outer edge and tuck the thread behind the needle before pulling through.

3. Repeat, stitching close to the first stitch on the inner circle, with wider spacing between stitches on the outer circle.

4. Continue the stitch. You create an arcing loop by inserting the needle very close to the previous stitch on the inner edge.

STITCHES FOR COVERAGE AND DETAILS

There are a few good ways to cover larger areas and to add small accents that will make your stitches really pop. For filling in spaces, variations of the satin stitch and herringbone stitch are the perfect fit, while French knots make ideal finishing touches.

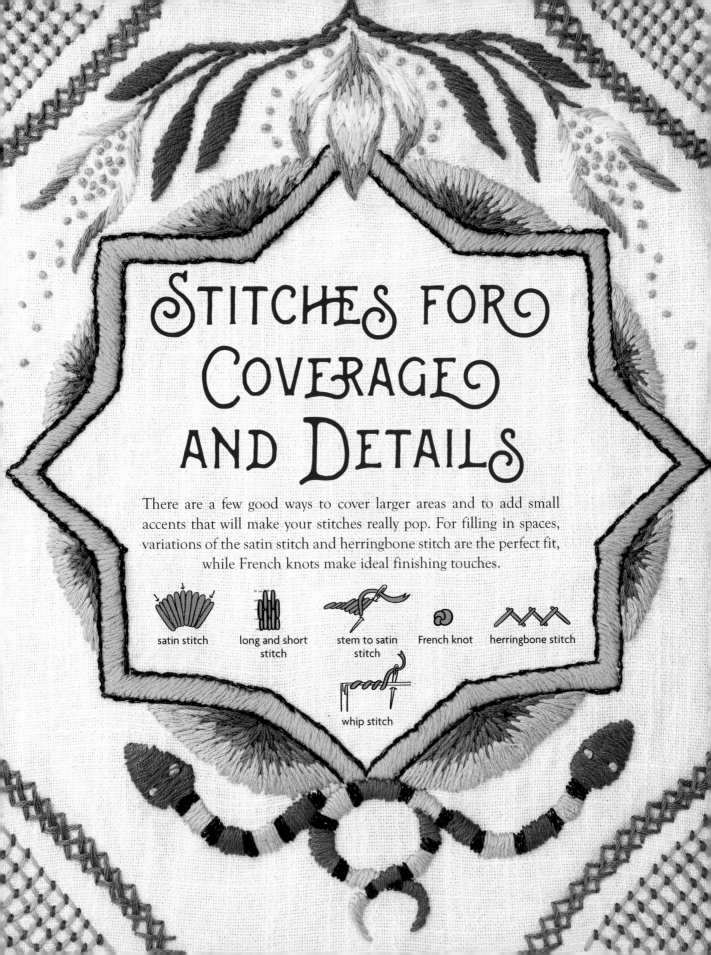

satin stitch

long and short stitch

stem to satin stitch

French knot

herringbone stitch

whip stitch

Satin Stitch

This works well for covering areas with smooth, uniform stitches. For wearable items, you want to keep the stitches under ½ inch long so they don't snag. The back of this stitch should look the same as the front. Consider the shape you will be filling with this stitch before you start, and which direction the stitches should go. The shorter the better!

1. Bring the needle out at one edge, and insert back in at the other edge, pulling through until the stitch is just a little bit raised. If you pull too tight, the tension will cause the fabric to pucker.

2. Insert the needle as close as possible to the previous stitch.

3. Continue, with the needle coming back up as close as possible to the previous stitch.

half stitches

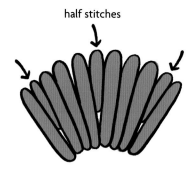

 TIP If you're creating a curved shape, like the color arcs in a rainbow for example, it helps to fill in the gaps on the wider edge of the arc with half stitches. This will help them blend in well visually.

Long and Short Stitch

This can be used to shade areas. By blending two or more colors together, it can also be used to fill in areas too large for a flat satin stitch in a single color. For example, a solid area that needs stitches longer than 1 inch is likely to get snagged. Instead, you can fill it in with this stitch while still achieving the beautiful texture of a satin stitch. This is not a stitch that requires perfection. A little randomness to the long and short can help to soften the texture.

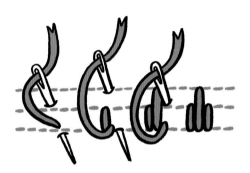 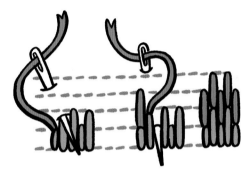

1. Begin your stitch on one edge of the area to be shaded, alternating between long and short satin stitches. The stitches should all line up on one edge, and the other edge will be staggered with long and short stitches. It may help to draw lines for each section of color, as shown in this example, creating rows about ¼ inch apart using an erasable marker or pencil as you learn this stitch.

2. On the next row (or in the next color if you're shading areas with multiple colors), split up through the end of the previously created stitches, then insert the needle two rows up. Bring the needle out by splitting up through the next stitch on the previous row. From here on, each stitch will be two "rows" long, which will stagger the edge and create a visual effect of blending the stitches.

3. Make long stitches of equal length, which will continue the staggered long-and-short effect. Continue this with as many colors as necessary, or as many rows as necessary if you're filling with a solid color.

 TIP If you're aiming for an even edge on the other side of the shaded area, finish with the same one-long, one-short stitches as the first row.

Stem to Satin Stitch

The angle of the stem stitch can transform into the thickness of a satin stitch, allowing you to move from a continuous line to filling in an area. For example, you can stitch a long stem with a leaf at the end, making a smooth transition between the two shapes.

1. To thicken the width of the stem stitch, slant the needle so it goes just to the side of the last stitch instead of in line with it.

2. Increase the amount of fabric taken up in each stitch, slanting the needle a little more each time to widen the area into a satin stitch.

3. As you slant the needle a little more, extend the length of each stitch a little beyond the length of the previous stitch.

 TIP If you wish to return to a stem stitch, slowly straighten out the slant with your next stitches.

French Knot

Use a French knot to create a pretty raised dot in your design.

1. After pulling the thread through to the front, wrap the thread around the needle very closely to the fabric (one wrap makes a small knot, two make a bigger knot), while pulling the loose end of the thread securely.

2. Insert the needle just a tiny bit from where the thread came out of the fabric, then pull through to the back.

   When creating French knots on top of a satin stitch or other filling stitches, you'll want to insert the needle about ⅛ inch from where the thread came out, tacking down an entire width of thread on the satin stitch so the French knot doesn't get lost in the stitches below.

3. Gently pull the thread all the way through, holding the knot down with your fingertip to keep it from tangling.

 TIP It may take a few tries to get the hang of this stitch. If the knot isn't staying, check that you are wrapping the needle from the eye toward the tip, and that the knot isn't pulling through the fabric to the back. If your knots continue to pull to the back, it may be because your fabric has a very open weave; try a bigger knot by wrapping the thread around the needle twice.

Herringbone Stitch

This fun detail for edgings, borders, and cuffs seems complex, but once you capture the rhythm, you'll find it stitches up quite quickly. Begin by drawing two parallel lines to mark the top and bottom edges of the stitch.

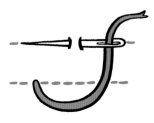  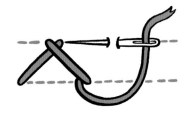

1. Bring the needle out on the left edge of the lower line. Insert the needle into the upper line a little to the right, creating a diagonal stitch. Then, with the needle facing the beginning of the line, bring its tip out about ⅛ inch away along the top line and pull through.

2. Crossing over the first diagonal stitch, insert the needle into the lower line a little to the right, then backstitch about ⅛ inch away on the bottom line and pull through.

3. Continue crossing over the previous stitch, creating a backstitch on the opposite line until the end.

 You can play with spacing here. Making the stitches closer together gives a denser effect; changing the angle of the diagonals gives you different options as well.

Grid Stitch

To fill in an area, create a square grid using straight stitches. Tack down each intersection with a single stitch (shown at the top of the illustration), making sure all tack stitches are going in the same direction. For a more pronounced effect, tack each intersection down with crossing stitches (shown on the left).

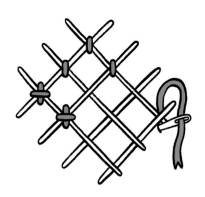

Whip Stitch

This technique is usually used as a seam joining two pieces of fabric together tightly, but it can also be a decorative element. By changing the length of the stitch, you can change the visual effect.

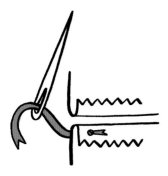 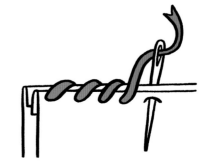

1. Fold ¼ inch of each edge you want to join toward the inside of the fabric (this is known as the seam allowance) and press the edge down with an iron or your fingernail. Thread the needle from inside to outside on one of the two pieces to be joined, close to the edge, so that the knot will be hidden on the inside of the seam.

2. With the thread coming out on the side of the fabric facing you, hold these two edges together with the seam allowance on the inside. Insert the needle into the back fabric, toward the side facing you (through both layers of the fabric) a little farther down the seam line, and pull through until the stitch lies flat, creating a diagonal stitch.

3. Repeat these diagonal stitches, keeping the stitch length consistent.

4

TREASURY OF SYMBOLS

The symbols collected here are especially meaningful to me. While many of them exist throughout the world in various forms, we are constantly re-creating, redesigning, and developing new ones. Any encyclopedia of symbols will always be, by nature, incomplete. You may know other forms that you want to work with. The more personal your association is, the stronger the effect it can have on your psyche. Sitting in meditation while holding an image mentally can also help bring up personal associations. Our experiences influence our definition of what a symbol means, so I urge you to build upon the descriptions I offer here with correspondences of your own. Feel free to combine these symbols, layer them, or dream up your own entirely. Stitching directions for all the symbols are provided in the stitch key in Chapter 7.

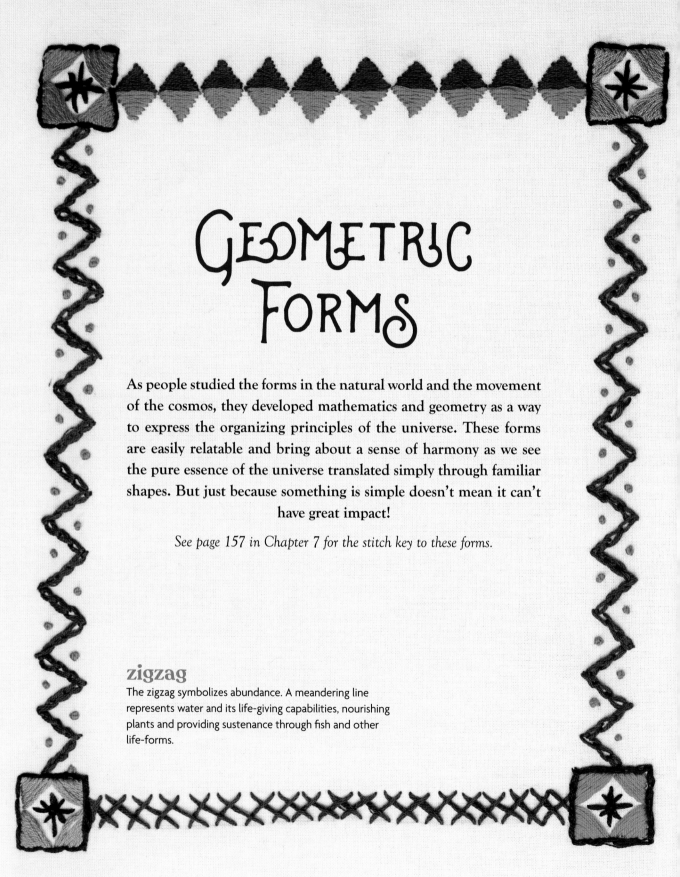

Geometric Forms

As people studied the forms in the natural world and the movement of the cosmos, they developed mathematics and geometry as a way to express the organizing principles of the universe. These forms are easily relatable and bring about a sense of harmony as we see the pure essence of the universe translated simply through familiar shapes. But just because something is simple doesn't mean it can't have great impact!

See page 157 in Chapter 7 for the stitch key to these forms.

zigzag

The zigzag symbolizes abundance. A meandering line represents water and its life-giving capabilities, nourishing plants and providing sustenance through fish and other life-forms.

STARS

Every culture has drawn stars in one form or another, and most relate them to concepts of illumination and divinity. As they twinkle in the sky, seemingly stationary yet always moving, the stars have come to represent the vastness of all that is, or the highest level of realization. They symbolize hope as it shines in the darkness, a constant where all else is transient.

five points

A visual illustration of the five elements in Traditional Chinese Medicine and in Western mysticism, the pentagram represents the spirit present within the human form. It's also used in Wiccan and modern pagan religions to call on the five elements for protection.

six points

Also known as the Seal of Solomon and the Shield of David, the upward and downward triangles signify the union of masculine and feminine. Though frequently appearing as a symbol of modern Judaism, it's been used decoratively by many religions throughout antiquity.

seven points

Known as the heptagram or septagram, this star was often used in alchemy (an ancient form of natural philosophy). It represented the seven days of creation and the seven planets of antiquity as they relate to the seven days of the week and the seven classical metals.

eight points

Closely related to the compass rose, this symbol can help you find your way. Also used as the Star of Lakshmi (two overlapping squares are a representation of the eight forms of the goddess) and the Star of Ishtar/Inanna (the Sumerian goddess of love and war).

half circle

In its resemblance to both the moon and a bowl or vessel, the half circle conveys a connection to the receptive feminine principle—cycles of nature, intuition, and inner mystery.

square

A symbol of support and structure. A sign of order and balance. It is also a sign of humanity, as many dwelling structures are based on this shape.

circle

A shape without corners, a circle is complete and self-contained. This is a visual representation of the number zero, pure potential, and the great cosmic egg.

cross

The intersection of the sacred and the mundane. The crossroads of Earth and the cosmos, and of the living and the dead. The vertical is cosmic and the horizontal is earthly.

wave

Wave is a sign of water, flow, and often grace. It represents the possibility for finding fluidity through change and movement.

arrow

A fast-moving energy directed toward a goal. The penetrating force of a warrior and the possibility for transcendence through swift action.

triangle

A visual representation of the number three—from the duality of two comes the unity of three. The trinity of divine, earth, and human—or mind, body, and soul.

spiral

A representation of the cyclical nature of life, but with its ever-expanding potential, the spiral expresses the necessity for evolution in these cycles. It illustrates the movement of creative forces spinning both outward and inward and is the most simple of labyrinths.

double helix

The geometric shape of our DNA closely resembles a spiraling ladder. The double helix has a close relationship to the winding serpents of the caduceus, an early symbol for medicine and healing.

hut

Found as far back as the Neolithic era and across many cultures, this is a sign of shelter and home. A roof overhead also serves as a symbol for coming together with family and community, and a sign of union and security.

mandorla

A fancy name for the shape created by two intersecting circles, this is also known as a vesica piscis. Resemblance to the shape of the vulva has given it meaning as a divine portal and representation of the act of creation.

lozenge

This is an archetypal depiction of the womb or the eye. In some Indigenous American cultures, this shape is created in yarn to symbolize the visions given through God (called nierika in Huichol traditions, and also known as God's eye). The eye is similarly used in Moroccan weavings.

chevron

These singular angled designs have been marked on human artwork dating back to the Neolithic era to represent birds flying through the sky, connecting the spirit world and earth. An upward-pointing chevron with a joining line was used to represent trees or snake spines, both signs of growth and potential.

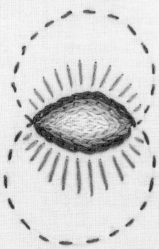

checkerboard

The dance of duality; this composition of alternating dark and light is an invitation to integrate our shadow aspects for a more complete understanding of our holistic self.

yin yang

An ancient Chinese symbol representing the complementary nature of opposing forces of the universe, the union of yin (feminine) energy and yang (masculine) energy. Within each is the seed of potential for the other, not able to exist without the balance of both.

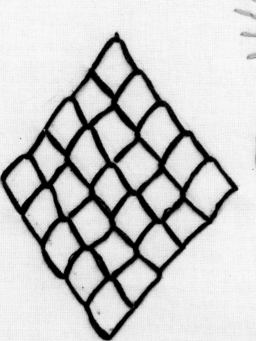

net

Representing one of the earliest tools of hunting, this pattern is found in artwork of early humans, presumably as a symbol of the life-giving powers of the goddess through a tool that provides sustenance. It can also be viewed in the larger context as a representation of the vast organizing principles that weave our fate.

ankh

A mysterious symbol from ancient Egypt thought to be the key to wisdom and a representation of combined masculine and feminine principles (much like the yin yang within us). More recent theories in Jungian psychology also reflect the importance of masculine and feminine powers working together for a complete and holistic self.

merkaba

Translated as "chariot" in Hebrew. The modern use of the word *merkaba* describes the combination of two tetrahedrons to create a three-dimensional star—a representation of our personal energy field through which we can transcend the material world. This symbolizes the opportunity for growth when we learn to work with spirit, mind, and body in unison.

philosopher's stone

An alchemical symbol of the ultimate quest to achieve unity or "spiritual gold," represented as the four elements of nature nestled in one another. Through the integration of all elements, we are able to achieve enlightenment.

triskelion

An ancient symbol of three spirals, sometimes shown as three legs, thought to bring luck and good fortune. Later adopted by Christianity as a visual representation of the Holy Trinity.

infinity

The eternal loop of life and death; an opportunity for renewal and transformation through ups and downs.

flower of life

A pattern of six overlapping circles found in artwork as early as the seventh century BCE, this is a representation of the divine pattern in all. The flower of life is a tessellation that can continue outward infinitely. In modern esoteric cultures, it has become a sign of harmony, the greater organizing principles of the universe, and our connection to all living things.

triple goddess

Three phases of the moon depict three forms of the goddess—a maiden in early years, mother in midlife, and wise crone in later years. This is often used in Wiccan symbolism and is a beautiful reminder of the value that lies in all stages of life, especially in a culture that tends to value youth.

PLATONIC SOLIDS

Stone versions of these solids found in Scotland have been dated to 4,000 years old, though their earliest known descriptions come from the writings of Plato (hence their name). These three-dimensional forms all have edges of equal length, sides of the same shape, and points each equidistant to the center. They each have a relation to one of the five elements of nature, and most of them can be found in the mineral kingdom in crystal forms.

See page 160 in Chapter 7 for the stitch key to these forms.

dodecahedron
Associated with ether or spirit, this shape is composed of 12 pentagons (five-sided polygons) and was said by Plato in one translation to be the form "which God used for embroidering the constellations on the whole heaven."

tetrahedron

Thanks to its sharp points, the simplest of the platonic forms was associated by Plato with the fire element, a symbol of rapid transformation. When viewed with the pointed angle facing forward, it appears to be three obtuse triangles though it is composed of four faces of equilateral triangles (all edges are the same length).

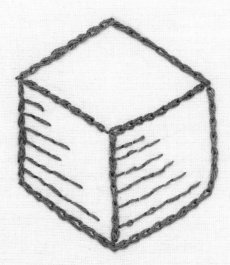

cube

This familiar form is associated with the earth element, sitting solidly on its base as a sign of stability. Composed of six square faces, when viewed from a diagonal angle it appears as a hexagon.

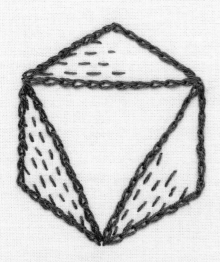

octahedron

This balance of shapes is associated with the element of air, a symbol of mental agility. Made of eight triangular sides, when viewed with one of the faces forward (as stitched here) it creates a hexagonal shape. When viewed facing one of its angles, it appears as a square with a cross through the middle.

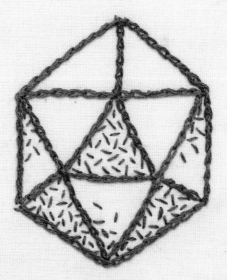

icosahedron

Made up of twenty equilateral triangles, this is the closest shape to a sphere in a triangular-based form. It is related to water and is a symbol of fluidity, literally going with the flow.

NUMBERS

Our mundane use of numbers as simple units of measure barely begins to tell their full story. Behind these integers lies a complex narrative of the basic elements of human experience. Numbers were our earliest method of discovering order in our lives. We can use numbers to strengthen our intentions and create a clearer message in our creative spellcasting.

See page 161 in Chapter 7 for the stitch key to these forms.

0

Both all and nothing; pure potential that is nearly impossible to describe without defying its own existence. Zero is a representation of the cosmic egg of possibility, the greatest mystery. Zero's symbolic nature as a circle could not be more appropriate, with no end and no beginning. It is a void, and therefore limitless and infinite.

1

Where life manifests, the spark of existence is found in One. It is the origin story and action taken, a sign of conception. The shape of the numeral rises upward as a symbol of its own active nature. In monotheistic religions it represents the creator. This potent number is the highest celestial power from which everything emerges.

2

Two is where we discover contrast. We are forced to find balance, to allow shadow and light to exist simultaneously. Two is where our subconscious dream worlds and intuition meet our rational, earthly selves. In some cultures, Two is considered the initial deviation from God and the origin of evil. However, if we recognize the inherent opposition in Two, we can allow its duality to be multifaceted, which is our most harmonious option.

3

The integer of creation; a synthesis or return to union after the split of Two. The trinity has many representations in religion and spirituality as the ultimate act of creation. In mythology, a trinity represents growth; from the duality of Two emerges a triad. The complete threefold power of divinity is represented as creation, preservation, and destruction.

4

In Four we find structure, control through logic, and the need to bring order and reason to our lives. The square is the building block of most weight-bearing forms; four corners on the ground represents our desire for stability.

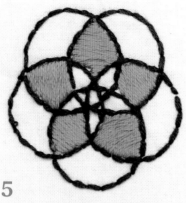

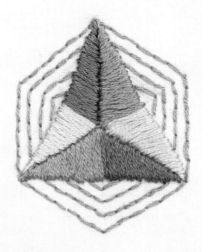

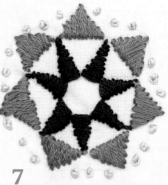

5

Asking us to transform, Five is where the four elements meet the changing nature of spirit. The opportunity is a complete transformation of self, our choice to see beyond the veil of physicality. It also relates to the five points of the human form as with the five-pointed star.

6

A feeling of harmony, Six is a number of union, choice, and free will. There is balance to be found in this quantity— a way to find equilibrium after the transformation we encountered in Five.

7

In Seven, we find spirit. From the freedom of choice in Six, we move to a driving force that comes from the higher self, an informed movement. We look to a greater picture. This odd number surrounds us in the alchemists' seven metals, the seven planets of antiquity, and the seven days of the week.

8

Moving past the perfect nature of Seven into the possibility beyond nature, Eight brings us to mastery, a return to balance and stability as we achieve higher knowledge. Relating to the minor points on a compass, Eight allows us to find our way to our own personal power and authority.

9

A sign of completion, having moved beyond the earthly world and the mastery of Eight into totally new territory, Nine brings us to the place where one story ends and another begins.

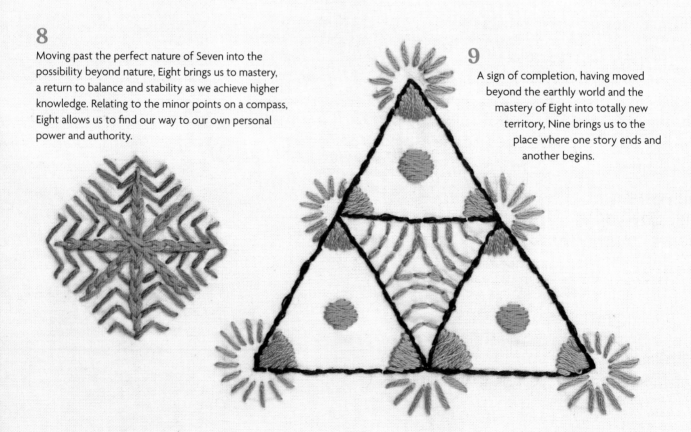

PLANETARY MAGIC

The orbiting bodies that dance around our galaxy have been studied since the beginning of humankind. Their ascribed traits come from millennia of observation of how their movements correlate to our lives on earth. In astrology, we use these cosmic forms to study or influence our personal interactions within the universe. We can also work with their archetypes—universal patterns and principles—and apply them to our lives. Whether or not you believe in astrology, the archetypes associated with each planet offer us a wonderful opportunity to channel divine energies in our daily experience.

See page 162 in Chapter 7 for the stitch key to these forms.

Venus

Sharing a name with the Roman goddess of love, Venus is a symbol of relationships, attraction, and pleasure. Its power can be channeled for romance and also for harmony among friends, family, and other communities. Venus also helps in accessing your own creativity and finding or creating more beauty in the world.

Mercury

Mercury is a symbol of communication and the active qualities of mind and body. Call on it for safe travels, successful correspondence, and contracts in business. It's also good for increasing mental activity, clear speech, better memory, and divination.

Earth

Our home planet, Earth is made of 70 percent water (same as the human heart and brain!) and nurtures the life-forms we know and love well. When in need of some grounding, or to "come down to earth," we can simply plant our feet on the dirt below us to channel this energy of home.

Saturn

With an energy of discipline, structure, and limitation, Saturn is not the most popular of planetary archetypes. Like that one person in a group who demands organization and responsibility, its energy is not much fun but very necessary for plans to work out smoothly. Saturn helps us channel our inner authority so we don't have to be governed by others. Working with Saturn can be a reality check; it helps get our lives in order and build a solid foundation to work from.

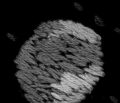

Mars

The red planet named for the Roman god of war, Mars is a planet of action and power. Assertive by nature, this energy of a courageous warrior can be channeled when firing up action or when you need victory in competition. Mars gets a bad reputation for being all about conflict and aggression, but when used for good in a balanced way, its energy can be highly valuable in getting the job done.

Sun

As the light of dawn that awakens us each morning, the radiance of the sun is energizing and purifying. Thinking of the sun as a symbol of strength and willpower, we can channel its energy when searching for vitality, courage, and good fortune. As our gardens grow abundantly in its light, it's also a great sign of prosperity.

Pluto

As governor of the cycle of life and death, Pluto gives us access to both destruction and renewal. It embodies the underworld qualities of life, the shameful parts of ourselves lurking in the shadows. We can choose to bring these dark qualities to the surface to be alchemized into our life's gold or allow them to destroy us from the inside out. Pluto cares not which path you choose but will be sure that transformation occurs either way.

Jupiter

Jupiter's gargantuan size lends it an identity as the planet of luck and expansion (you can fit 1,321 Earths inside this behemoth!). Call upon this planet of abundance in matters of ambition and success. It is also associated with philosophical ideas and intellectual growth. Be warned, however, that unchecked growth and overindulgence are not always good things, so know your limits.

Uranus

Uranus is the revolutionary of the solar system, questioning the status quo. The first of the "outer planets," Uranus is an archetype of unconventional ideas, original concepts, freedom, and rebellion. Both the breakthrough and the breakdown, it blows up our idea of the way things "should" be. When we ignore the need for transformation in our lives, Uranus is the energy that forces us to change, often in ways that feel disruptive.

Neptune

In a liminal realm where imagination rules, Neptune allows us to access our deepest dreams and intuition. This archetype offers opportunity to connect with the spiritual but can also tend toward escapism. We can use it in ways that are healing and life-affirming, or we can fall into the trap of illusion. A source of creative illumination when you find yourself in a space lacking that divine spark, Neptune can help you find a path through myth, spirituality, and other unseen forces.

MOON PHASES

The moon is our satellite and our most visible keeper of time as it reflects the light of our sun. This glowing body completes its orbit around our planet every 28 days and throughout this cycle passes through phases of light and dark as viewed from Earth. You can choose to work with the phases of the moon as you craft your designs. For example, creating a talisman for abundance or attracting something would best be done on the waxing moon. Creating a talisman for releasing or letting go of something might be more effective when made during the waning moon. The detailed craters of the moon can also be a joy to embroider!

See page 163 in Chapter 7 for the stitch key to these forms.

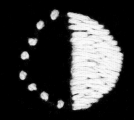

first quarter

As the moon's glowing surface grows and its force on the Earth's tides becomes stronger, we experience energy flowing more freely. Attraction and action come with greater ease.

waxing crescent

This shining crescent rises during the morning hours and sets before midnight. This is a time to take into account what you need to nurture your intentions.

new

The new moon is barely visible—a tiny silver slice rising at dawn and setting at sunset. This is a time that supports the exploration of new possibilities, setting intentions, and developing plans for your month ahead.

full

This is the halfway point of the lunar cycle, when light is shed on our dreams and on the intentions we set at the new moon. This can be a great time for release in both physical and emotional realms—clean your house or cry your heart out, your choice! Also good for joining up with community in the light of the evening.

waxing gibbous

We catch this phase shining into our windows in the evening; it calls us outside to see its glorious reflection and claim the intense power available.

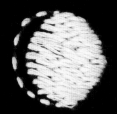

waning gibbous

This is a more internal period of release. Ask yourself what you can change from within as you move through the darkening of the moon cycle. It's a wonderful time to uncover what you feel might need adjustment in your life.

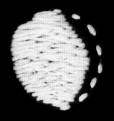

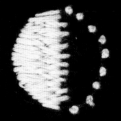

last quarter

As the light cast on the moon each night begins to wane, we are called to continue letting go of what we no longer need. This includes deep-seated habits and tendencies as well as physical clutter.

waning crescent

The dark period before the new moon is a time that supports clearing out any leftover cobwebs. It is also a great time to meditate on the most supportive ways to work with the coming new moon.

Zodiac Signs

The zodiac is much more than an interpretation of personality type based on our date of birth. A symbolic map of the stars as they relate to our time orbiting the sun, these 12 signs have long been a part of our human history and integral in astronomical research. Much like the planets, each sign of the zodiac carries an archetype that is thought to correlate to our experiences on Earth. You don't have to stick to your birth sign; I find astrological signs to be helpful in channeling archetypes I'd like to bring into my life. If I'm wishing for more community and conversation, I work with the sign of Gemini to channel this quality. Working with these archetypes is a way to describe our intentions captured in one symbol, rather than try to stitch a number of disparate desires. The signs and their qualities are based on the time of year in the Northern Hemisphere, as Europe is the birthplace of modern Western astrology.

See page 164 in Chapter 7 for the stitch key to these forms.

Aries

The first sign of the zodiac brings a fiery initiatory quality that can infuse a new project with enthusiasm and vigor. Represented by the ram, an active animal of power, Aries is ruled by the planet Mars and is related to the renewal of the sun in the early spring.

Taurus

Practical and stable, the second sign of the zodiac is grounded in the earth and known for a love of beauty. Symbolized by the bull, a strong and stubborn animal, yet ruled by the planet Venus, this sign manages to be both sensual and sensible.

Gemini

The twins representing this sign reflect the dual nature of humanity, coupled with the intellectual quickness of a lively discussion, evident in its ruling planet, Mercury. This is a sign of expression and communication but can be susceptible to flightiness.

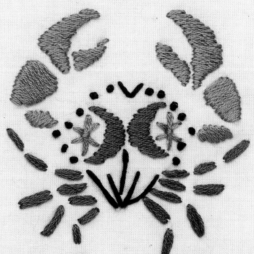

Cancer

The sign of home and family, the crab is an animal that carries its own hard-shelled home with it. Ruled by the moon, Cancer manages to ground the watery qualities of emotion and intuition with care and discipline.

Leo

The strength and vigor of the lion projects an inner fierceness backed by its ruling celestial body, the sun. Leo's fiery enthusiasm can tend toward boastful, but there's an inherent determination and inspiring courage to this summer sign.

Virgo

Symbolized by the virgin, a term that originally meant a "woman unto herself" and had nothing to do with sexual experience, Virgo is the sign of the earth mother whose harvest is rich. Ruling planet Mercury (which also rules Gemini) offers critical practicality.

Libra

A sign of justice and diplomacy symbolized by the balanced scales, Libra seeks what is most fair. Ruled by the planet Venus, this pull toward equality is joined with an appetite for beauty in all forms.

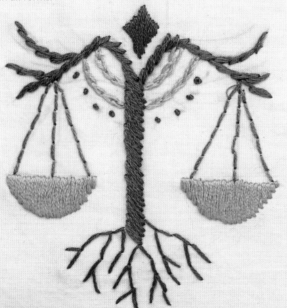

Scorpio

Represented by the scorpion (as well as the eagle, phoenix, and serpent), which often symbolizes destruction, this sign is considered intense because those born under it seek to get to the core truth of a situation quickly. Scorpio is ruled by Pluto and related to the winter season, which invites us to face the concept of death as a necessary element of life on Earth.

Sagittarius

Sometimes represented as the archer, or as the half-man, half-horse centaur, Sagittarius is a symbol of an enthusiastic desire for expansion. Ruled by Jupiter, and emerging at the time of the year that coincides with the hunt, this sign embodies a desire to seek new lands and ideas.

Capricorn

An expressive quality combines with ambition and a desire to do things the "right" way in this creature that is half-goat, half-fish. Saturn leads this sea-goat into action no matter what the challenges—and in the depths of winter, this is a desirable trait!

Aquarius

While known to be community oriented and socially invested, this sign isn't swayed by the crowd. The ruling planet Uranus grants this water bearer offbeat and eccentric qualities. It is not a sign ruled by emotion; holding the water vessel signifies holding control over the watery realms.

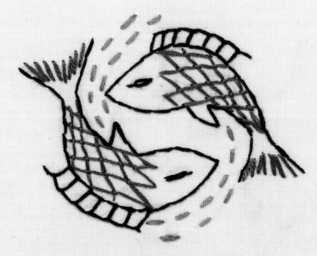

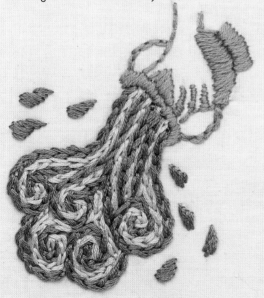

Pisces

With a dreamy sensitivity, fish immerse themselves deep in the qualities of their ruling planet, Neptune. They swim in either direction, and as the final sign of the zodiac, their movement symbolizes coming and going, past and future.

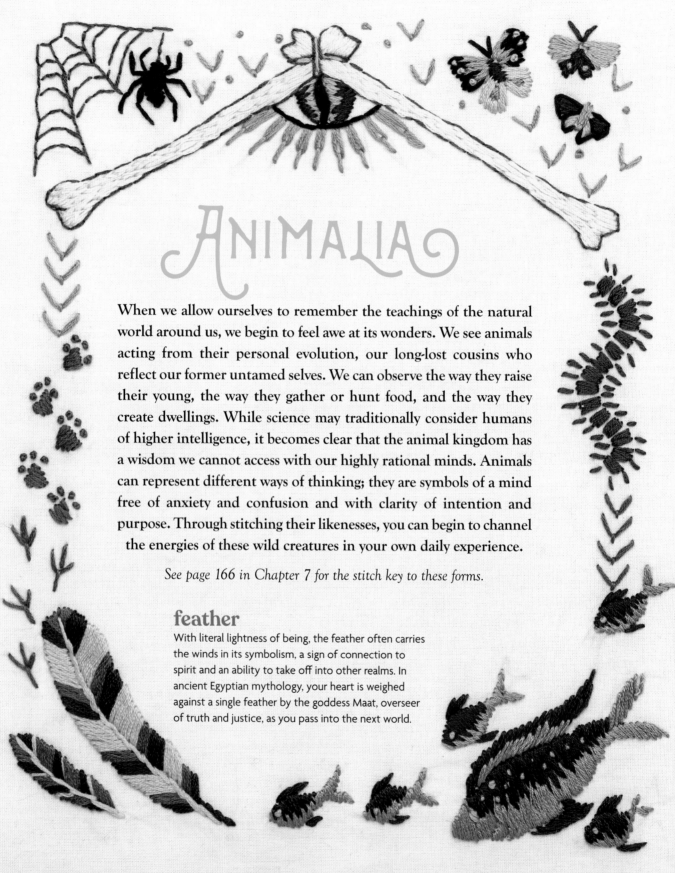

Animalia

When we allow ourselves to remember the teachings of the natural world around us, we begin to feel awe at its wonders. We see animals acting from their personal evolution, our long-lost cousins who reflect our former untamed selves. We can observe the way they raise their young, the way they gather or hunt food, and the way they create dwellings. While science may traditionally consider humans of higher intelligence, it becomes clear that the animal kingdom has a wisdom we cannot access with our highly rational minds. Animals can represent different ways of thinking; they are symbols of a mind free of anxiety and confusion and with clarity of intention and purpose. Through stitching their likenesses, you can begin to channel the energies of these wild creatures in your own daily experience.

See page 166 in Chapter 7 for the stitch key to these forms.

feather

With literal lightness of being, the feather often carries the winds in its symbolism, a sign of connection to spirit and an ability to take off into other realms. In ancient Egyptian mythology, your heart is weighed against a single feather by the goddess Maat, overseer of truth and justice, as you pass into the next world.

earthworm

This spineless creature who lives in the earth is seen as a sign of humility. When we look a little closer, we can see its acts of service. As the worm breaks down organic matter, it transforms what seems like garbage or dirt into a life-sustaining material that is required for every living thing.

moth or butterfly

Transmutation of the soul is often symbolized by the cocoon or chrysalis, the ultimate alchemical vessel of transformation. The metamorphosis from egg to caterpillar to cocoon/chrysalis to flight makes a powerful metaphor for emergence from your own flightless primordial soup into an uplifting form, able to take flight despite any resistance.

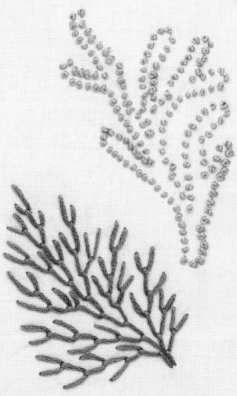

coral

Once thought to be a plant, coral is actually composed of colonies of marine invertebrate polyps that over time create the skeletal formations we see. Coral has taken on a variety of meanings throughout history and cultures, from a symbol of the fertility of the sea to protection during life passages (revealed by its discovery in ancient Egyptian tombs). Given what we now know about coral, its representation as harmonious group energy seems the most appropriate!

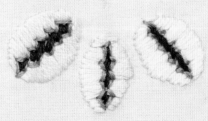

fish

These radiant beings covered in iridescent scales were one of the first species to evolve from simpler forms of life. Their lidless eyes reflect the all-seeing nature of God (in both alchemy and Christianity), and their ease with being immersed in the watery depths offers us a connection to the deep waters of our own inner worlds.

cowrie shell

Representing fertility of the great mother ocean, the cowrie's vulvalike shape makes it easy to see a connection with feminine powers of creation. It has been used as currency in many areas (including West African countries, India, and China) and symbolizes wealth.

owl

Hunting in the dark hours of night, with its giant eyes and rotating head, the owl has brought associations with darkness, death, and peering beyond the light of day. It's also related to wisdom and guidance through spirit realms. Work with the owl to help you see in the dark, connect with night, and find wisdom in dark times.

hawk

Soaring at the highest of heights, the hawk is the warrior of the sky, with giant talons, a sharp beak, and even sharper eyesight. Related to the sun, the hawk can offer the ability to view a situation from afar with new and keen perception.

dove

A symbol of eternal love, the dove is a display of peace and tranquility, thanks to its docile nature. Allow this delicate beauty to bring serenity and love into your life situations.

raven

A prophetic bird, the raven is highly intelligent and mischievous and has the unusual ability to make tools. Humans have long associated birds with being messengers from the spirit realm, and because ravens consume the remains of death they have been considered messengers of the underworld. Allow raven to assist in communion with spirits and those who have passed on.

egg

A magical emblem of life, and a sign of possibility and ultimate potential, the egg has found a place in creation myths around the world. Nestled within the egg is the potential for life. All that exists is said to have emerged from the cosmic egg.

swan

One of many birds who mate for life, swans are especially tied to love and fidelity. They are also the birds that pull the chariot of Venus, goddess of love. It is said that they sing the most beautiful song just before death, so they draw an association with contentment in passage. Work with the swan for grace in love, with a touch of fierceness.

wing

Popular in Western and Middle Eastern mythology, wings are a sign of communication between humankind and the gods. Used ritually to send offerings of sweetly scented incense up to the heavens, the wing is a symbolic intermediary of sorts and also a wish for safe travels.

bird claw

Used by birds to grab prey, the claw is thought to provide the strength and cunning needed for a successful hunt. In some spiritual practices of the African diaspora such as Hoodoo, chicken claws are a talisman of protection, as they can scratch out any evil that may come your way.

antler

The virility and power of a mature male deer is channeled in this arching crown (though in the case of reindeers, both males and females grow antlers). As cultures relied on deer for sustenance and, in some climates, deer shed their antlers seasonally, deer can also serve as a symbol for the cycle of life, death, rebirth, and regeneration.

nautilus

A divine form that reflects the sacred spiral, the nautilus shell displays the golden ratio of mathematical forms. Allow this perfection of nature to remind you of your own divine essence.

oyster and pearl

The oyster is a symbol of the creative and generative powers of the womb, as it was once thought to nurture the shimmering pearl. Historically, the pearl was a symbol of divine essence and perfection. Now that we know how pearls are created—the oyster's immune system reacts to irritating foreign objects by covering them with an iridescent coating—the pearl has become a symbol of the beauty that emerges out of challenging or troublesome situations.

conch

This spiral form is found in the ancient myths of Greek, Indian, and Aztec societies and was also used as a musical instrument or as a vessel to hold holy waters. The conch shell symbolizes an opportunity to connect with the deep wisdom and beauty of the ocean.

bee

Creators of sweet golden nectar blessed by the sun and flowers, these industrious creatures can be called upon when you want to create sweetness with your labor. They're also connected to the deceased; in some cultures, it's believed that the soul leaves the body in the form of bees or that bees lead the newly dead to rest in peace.

scarab

The dung beetle, most sacred of all scarabs, lays its eggs in a ball of dung. As it wheels these dung balls up the dunes, like the sun climbs each morning, the scarab serves as a great symbol for birthing new projects that you've been diligently rolling along with.

spider

Spinning weaver of the insect world and role model of the textile arts, the spider's creations give form to her silent hunt. She teaches us to approach our tasks from the perspective of increasing our skills with patience.

salamander

Thought to be born out of flames, the salamander is a sign of enduring faith through the fires of temptation. It works well for calling on courageous swiftness.

serpent

Creator and destroyer, no animal quite captures the human imagination like the serpent. Dualistic by nature, the serpent is simultaneously a cold-blooded subterranean dweller and a sun-loving creature that emerges from the depths to shed its skin and begin anew. Winding their way through mythology and folklore worldwide, serpents appear as a force of evil and temptation as well as wisdom and fertility. They are a symbol of transformation, renewal, and the cyclical nature of existence.

wolf

The Roman myth of creation tells of Romulus and Remus suckling from an adoptive wolf mother. The wolf is a sign of our deep connection to our animal instincts and to our savage tendencies rooted in nature.

bear

Massive and protective, the bear is a symbol of courage and leadership, with its combination of spirit and strength. After hibernation, the bear digs up osha root to revive its system in spring. The bear's use of valuable medicinal herbs has associated it with the power of healing.

ant

Small yet industrious and determined, ants represent the power of an organized community in action. Hordes of these insects can consume dead bodies or build towering forms. Their ability to simultaneously create order and chaos offers a sign of how our tiny actions have the power to move mountains.

big cats

Silently slinking, waiting for just the right moment to pounce on prey, big cats exhibit a fierce elegance you're lucky to catch a glimpse of. They are a sign of swift grace.

stingray

The ray's gentle and graceful form seems to dance through the ocean. It is beautiful, yet it can also be dangerous when necessary. The ray's movements imply harmony as well as a refusal to be walked all over—a balance we can all use some support in finding.

octopus

One of the most mysterious creatures of the deep ocean, the octopus can shape-shift to fit into the tiniest space; and when a tentacle breaks off, another grows in its place. Octopuses are incredibly intelligent and known to cause destruction in aquariums, making them an ideal choice for finding your own sneaky mystery.

mouse

Fast moving, skilled at hiding, and nearly imperceptible, the tiny mouse has been vilified for its harm to humans, spreading disease and destroying crops. Mice serve as a sign of clever determination and remind us that the accumulation of tiny deeds can have great effects.

rabbit

In addition to reproducing at an incredible rate, rabbits are also flirtatious in their mating process, making them a sign of fertility and playfulness. They eat at dawn and dusk (transitional times of day), and are associated with the moon in both Chinese and Aztec mythology. They're also known as a trickster in some Indigenous cultures of North America.

deer

Respected for their calm and graceful demeanor, deer draw the chariot of the maiden goddess of the hunt, Artemis. Call on deer to bring gentle grace into your life.

frog

Emerging from fertile waters, the tadpole serves as a symbol of resurrection and transformation. A frog's squatting position has historically represented childbirth and, considering the vast number of offspring frogs produce, their association with fertility is quite appropriate!

sea turtle

Guided by the light of the moon, sea turtles emerge from the ocean to lay their eggs on the beach. As soon as an egg hatches, the baby must hurry to the sea to survive being picked off by predatory birds. Breathing air and living in water, the sea turtle is quite the intermediary. Mythology in Iroquois, Chinese, and Hindu traditions all tell of the world growing on a turtle shell. Allow the energy of these long-lived creatures to help support your own dreams of longevity.

elephant

Though generally gentle in nature, the elephant is a fierce protector when provoked. Elephants form matriarchal societies and display grandiose authority while also tending to community, which makes them a beautiful symbol for gracious leadership and wisdom.

Mythical Beasts

Visions of furred and feathered beasts with otherworldly powers emerged from the depths of the human psyche millennia ago and have fascinated us ever since. Many of these creatures have traveled the globe and crossed cultures through oral tradition and shared mythologies. Often an amalgamation of real creatures, mythical beasts reference and reinvent well-known animals in imaginative ways that can delight and frighten us. Invite these supernatural forms into your process for assistance in telling a grandiose and otherworldly story.

See page 171 in Chapter 7 for the stitch key to these forms.

phoenix

The phoenix dies in a glorious flame. A sign of resurrection and rebirth, it is born anew from its own ashes and then offers the ashes to the altar of the sun god. This is a symbol of personal transformation, burning off the old and entering into a new form with appreciation for your former self.

winged horse

These often symbolize the immortal nature of the soul. The most popular is Pegasus, who can produce water springs by stamping his hoof. In Greek mythology, Pegasus is ridden each morning by Eos, goddess of the dawn, to bring the sun to the sky. Allow the winged horse to bring the light of dawn to your experience.

sphinx

Keepers of mystery, the Egyptian sphinx was usually male and a sign of royalty and wisdom, while the Greek sphinx was depicted as female and more complex in meaning, often questioning travelers with a riddle. Both are guardians known for their strength and intelligence. What will you ask the sphinx to guard for you?

dragon

Bird meets serpent and strength meets wisdom at the mouth of the dragon's lair. Western history requires dragons to be slain, but Eastern culture views them as intermediaries between gods and humans. How will this flying form reveal the hidden knowledge you seek?

unicorn

A modern symbol of the unique and rare, the unicorn's history is actually multidimensional. The horn was said to be a panacea, while the animal was a sign of purity, especially a sexually pure virgin.

hydra

The multiheaded snake guarded the entrance to the underworld in Greek mythology and was ultimately destroyed by Hercules. Hindu illustrations of Vishnu and Lakshmi on the cosmic sea also depict a multi-headed cosmic snake named Ananta as a sign of alertness accessible through meditation. The hydra offers an opportunity to explore what needs to be slain or tamed in order to move forward in life.

griffin

Combining the courage of a lion and the keen eye of the eagle, the griffin serves as a powerful protector and guardian of treasures. Griffins have been employed as a symbol of military power in Europe, though this association is of ancient Iranian origin. Can this fierce protector help you defend your own priceless treasures?

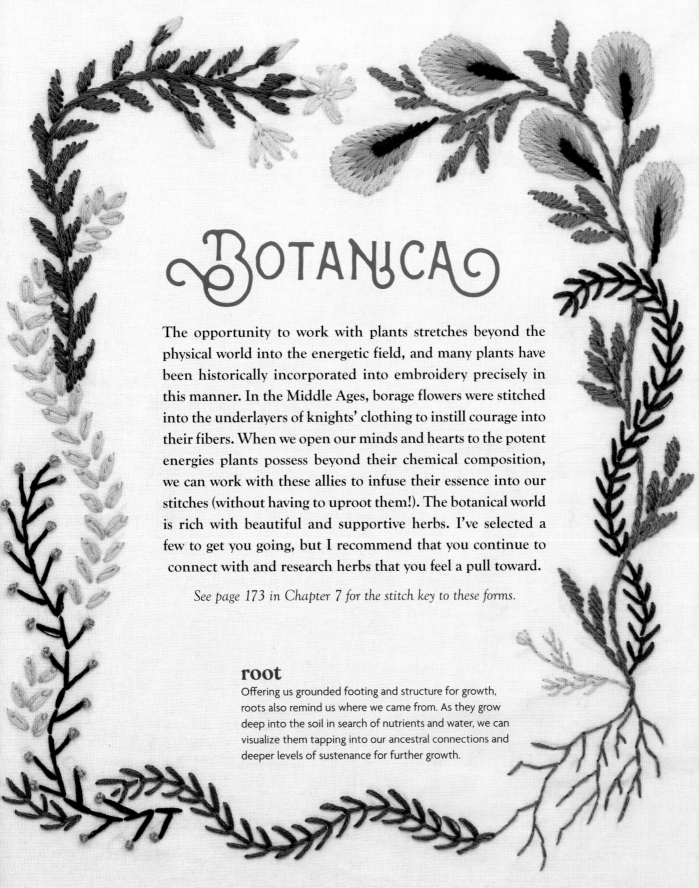

BOTANICA

The opportunity to work with plants stretches beyond the physical world into the energetic field, and many plants have been historically incorporated into embroidery precisely in this manner. In the Middle Ages, borage flowers were stitched into the underlayers of knights' clothing to instill courage into their fibers. When we open our minds and hearts to the potent energies plants possess beyond their chemical composition, we can work with these allies to infuse their essence into our stitches (without having to uproot them!). The botanical world is rich with beautiful and supportive herbs. I've selected a few to get you going, but I recommend that you continue to connect with and research herbs that you feel a pull toward.

See page 173 in Chapter 7 for the stitch key to these forms.

root

Offering us grounded footing and structure for growth, roots also remind us where we came from. As they grow deep into the soil in search of nutrients and water, we can visualize them tapping into our ancestral connections and deeper levels of sustenance for further growth.

apple

Ripening just in time for All Hallow's Eve (Halloween), this juicy red fruit is a sign of the changing of seasons, preparing us for descent into winter's darkness. The apple can be seen as an invitation to discover sweetness in the dark shadows, or, in the case of Adam and Eve, falling into suffering through the knowledge of good and evil. The choice is yours.

seed

Each seed holds within it the possibility for innumerable future plants. This unlimited potential for growth from such a tiny form reminds us what an impact something so small can have.

wheat

A foundational part of the human diet in many cultures, an abundance of wheat has come to symbolize wealth and fertility in all areas of life.

sage

An herb of protection and wisdom, garden sage and white sage have both been burned as purifying incense. Known to cleanse the mind and soothe the stomach, sage leaves can be stitched when you are in need of tranquility.

mushroom

Running underground is a mysterious network of fungi, called mycelium, connecting all plants in the surrounding area. The mystical and beautiful forms that show up aboveground as clusters of charming toadstools are a part of this system. Finding life in decomposition, allowing the death of one to feed another, they support the entire community and remind us of the interconnectedness of all.

calendula

This herb of the sun is extremely healing when used topically. Work with calendula for prosperity in both the material and spiritual worlds, as it is considered a visionary herb. Choose this bloom to light up your life with its healing presence.

marigold

From wedding garlands in India to funerary adornment in Mexico, marigold has provided bright blooms in times of major life transitions. Allow this classic garden bloom to support the changing of forms we regularly face throughout our lives.

dandelion

No other plant is quite as prolific as the common dandelion, condemned as a weed yet never ceasing to shine its glowing blossom to the sky. Such endurance makes the dandelion a beautiful choice for manifesting prosperity and good fortune.

red clover

These delicate puffs of petals help cleanse the blood and clear coughs. Red clover is known to support healthy soil (by fixing nitrogen) and healthy blood. Energetically, it supports healthy relationships and has historically been included in love spells.

rosemary

Burned as a cleansing and protective incense, this herb clears the energy of a space and provides clarity of mind. Rosemary also supports memory and remembrance with a connection to the dead and a peaceful afterlife. Soothing to the nervous system, it is often included in love spells.

mugwort

The pale underside of this leafy herb hints at its lunar essence; mugwort works to enhance vivid dreaming and soothe worn muscles. Its dried leaves have been burned in support of astral travels. Try working with mugwort's energies for active dreaming supported by the cycles of the moon.

lily

The lily has been a representation of innocence and purity, and historically related to mothers and children. Symbolizing the virtuous nature of the Virgin Mary in Christianity, lilies are also seen as a flower of protection and harmony. Choose this bloom to bring the light of innocence to your workings.

goldenrod

The ability to reproduce through drifting blooms and rambling roots makes these spikes of glowing yellow sparks the epitome of abundance; they have been thought to help one find fortune. Stitch a few for good luck and prosperity.

yarrow

Said to have grown from the wound on Achilles' heel, this abundant blossom has been used in love charms and for magical purposes. It has a role in both wound healing and love bringing. Allow this rich medicine to help in your quest for love and be your salve for any hurt you may incur in the process.

poppy

The flower that blooms before becoming the opium seed, the poppy has been related to the night and deep sleep. A sign of remembrance for the dead, the herb is also used as a delicate sedative. Energetically, the image of its bloom can help to support release and surrender.

rose

With its powerful beauty and scent carefully guarded by its thorns, this sacred bloom has held symbolism in most cultures as a sign of love and devotion, as well as for divination. Work with the wild rose as a symbol of harmony in love or for finding direction on your path to love.

peony

Though its glorious blooms are short-lived, the peony emerges from the ground in early spring and grows at a rapid pace signaling good fortune and abundance. The seeds and roots were historically used for protection from evil, strung into beads and worn similar to a rosary.

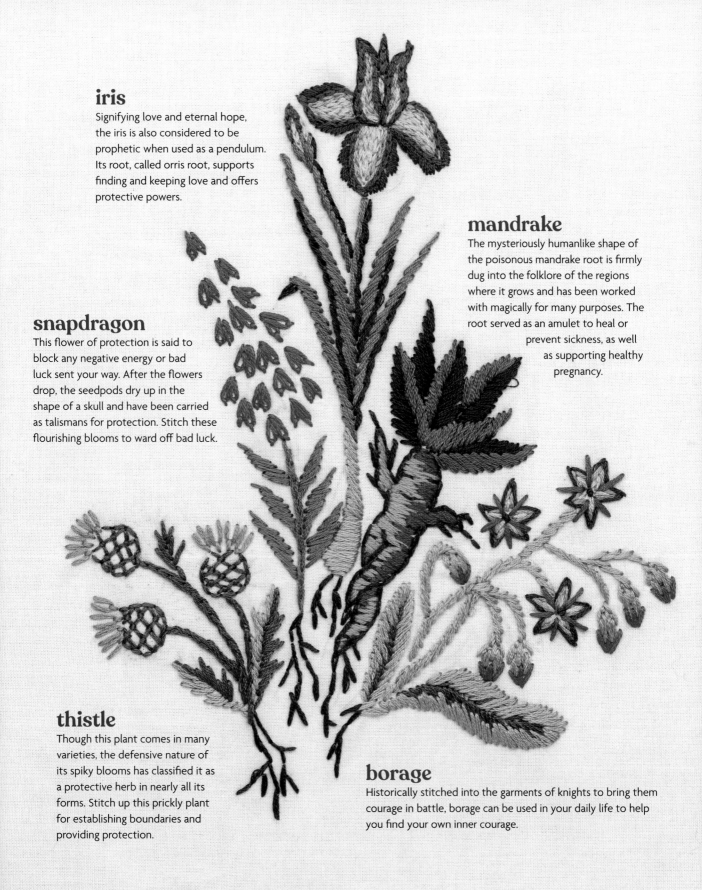

iris

Signifying love and eternal hope, the iris is also considered to be prophetic when used as a pendulum. Its root, called orris root, supports finding and keeping love and offers protective powers.

mandrake

The mysteriously humanlike shape of the poisonous mandrake root is firmly dug into the folklore of the regions where it grows and has been worked with magically for many purposes. The root served as an amulet to heal or prevent sickness, as well as supporting healthy pregnancy.

snapdragon

This flower of protection is said to block any negative energy or bad luck sent your way. After the flowers drop, the seedpods dry up in the shape of a skull and have been carried as talismans for protection. Stitch these flourishing blooms to ward off bad luck.

thistle

Though this plant comes in many varieties, the defensive nature of its spiky blooms has classified it as a protective herb in nearly all its forms. Stitch up this prickly plant for establishing boundaries and providing protection.

borage

Historically stitched into the garments of knights to bring them courage in battle, borage can be used in your daily life to help you find your own inner courage.

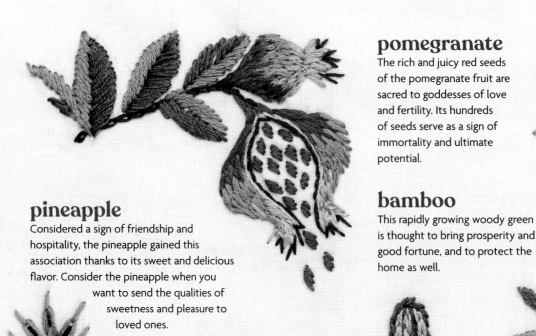

pomegranate

The rich and juicy red seeds of the pomegranate fruit are sacred to goddesses of love and fertility. Its hundreds of seeds serve as a sign of immortality and ultimate potential.

pineapple

Considered a sign of friendship and hospitality, the pineapple gained this association thanks to its sweet and delicious flavor. Consider the pineapple when you want to send the qualities of sweetness and pleasure to loved ones.

bamboo

This rapidly growing woody green is thought to bring prosperity and good fortune, and to protect the home as well.

saguaro cactus

The cactus's ability to grow in harsh climates has made it a symbol of thriving no matter what the circumstances. Work with this prickly friend for support through dry times.

palm

Upward reaching, fruit bearing, and vibrant green, the palm has been a symbol of fertility and a bountiful harvest, and later, by Christians, of pilgrimage. Work with this symbol for active abundance.

lotus

Serving as a representation of the chakras in Indian systems, the many petals of the lotus gently reveal its layered symbolism. The lotus's graceful elegance growing in muddy waters serves as a sign of our own human potential for beauty within a world of chaos.

bay laurel

An herb of wisdom, the kind gained through education and also through clairvoyance, bay laurel has found its place in symbolism since at least ancient Grecian times. Wreaths of laurel are still used today as a crown of triumph in athletics. When burned, laurel's volatile oils spark quite magically and have been used as a purification and visionary incense.

cedar

Incense from the wood and the leaves of this evergreen have been used for their purifying and protective energies. Due to their ability to stay green through harsh winters, most evergreens are also considered to draw abundance.

juniper

Offering protection by attracting positive energies and repelling unhealthful ones, this evergreen has the added benefit of berries that support virility and the attraction of lovers.

white pine

Considered the "tree of peace," white pine grows exclusively in North America and has been of immense importance to Indigenous peoples. Nourishing and healing, the inner bark was used for flour in times when food was scarce, and the resin worked both for waterproofing and for salving wounds.

oak

A tree of great importance both in Indigenous American and in Celtic traditions, the oak is a sign of longevity, durability, and fertility. Its acorns present themselves in abundance as a valuable food source and have served as a staple in the diet of many cultures.

maple

While there are quite a few species of this hardy tree, the sweetness of its sap and its ability to thrive in most places make it a great choice as a symbol of enduring growth.

FORCES OF NATURE

The original artist, designer, and manufacturer of only the finest goods, nature is the source of us, of all we know, and of all we can imagine. Nature's majestic forms have served as the source of inspiration for as long as we have existed. We are nothing without nature because we are, in fact, part of nature. The movements of the sky, the stable earth below our feet, and everything in between have inexhaustible wisdom to teach us.

See page 177 in Chapter 7 for the stitch key to these forms.

mountain

Rising up toward the cosmos, the peak has always been considered a source of divine inspiration. The ascent up a mountain provides opportunity for spiritual growth and serves as a sign of the monumental nature of earthly powers. Allow these forms to represent transcendence, movement beyond the mundanities of human life.

cloud

These formations in the sky provide the gift of rain yet also conceal the mystery of the cosmos above. Their presence can be a sign of compassion or a bringer of great storms, connecting them closely to the spirit world. Consider stitching some clouds as a symbol of the thin veil between the celestial spirits and our earthly lives.

lightning

Striking down to the earth, a bolt of lightning emerges from the darkened skies like a visit from the celestial realm. Bring this symbol in to call on swift action and to illuminate enlightening messages from the skies above.

droplet

The rain, the dew, a tear. These forms of moving water are all a symbol of release and of the fertile and supportive nature of water, whether nourishing plants or allowing our emotions to flow.

river

The endless nature of a river serves to signify the flow of our own lives. The image of a river supports abundance as its waters provide a home for so much life and a source of sustenance for the plants and animals that live near it.

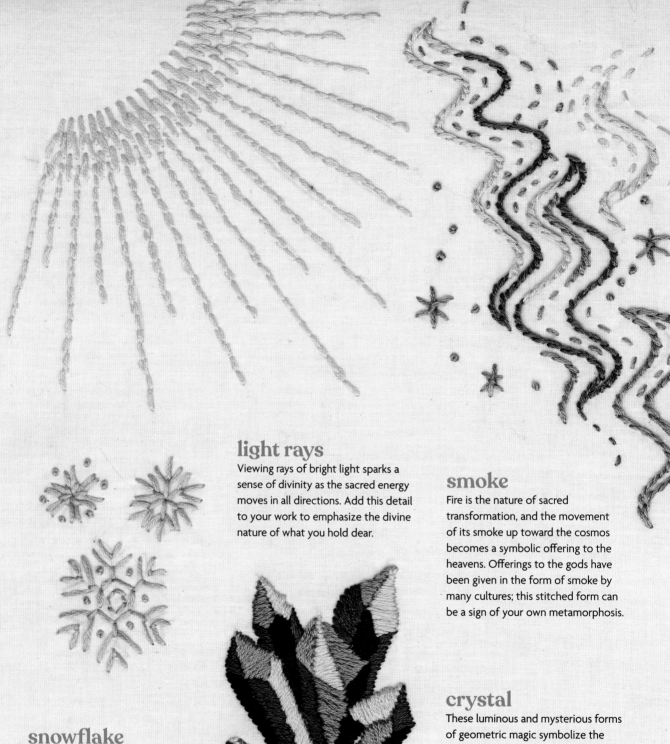

light rays

Viewing rays of bright light sparks a sense of divinity as the sacred energy moves in all directions. Add this detail to your work to emphasize the divine nature of what you hold dear.

smoke

Fire is the nature of sacred transformation, and the movement of its smoke up toward the cosmos becomes a symbolic offering to the heavens. Offerings to the gods have been given in the form of smoke by many cultures; this stitched form can be a sign of your own metamorphosis.

crystal

These luminous and mysterious forms of geometric magic symbolize the divine powers held deep in the earth's core. While they come in many shapes and sizes, they never cease to amaze and inspire with their eye-catching structure and glittering light.

snowflake

During the harsh depths of winter, the geometrically perfect form of each individual snowflake serves as creative inspiration delivered directly from above.

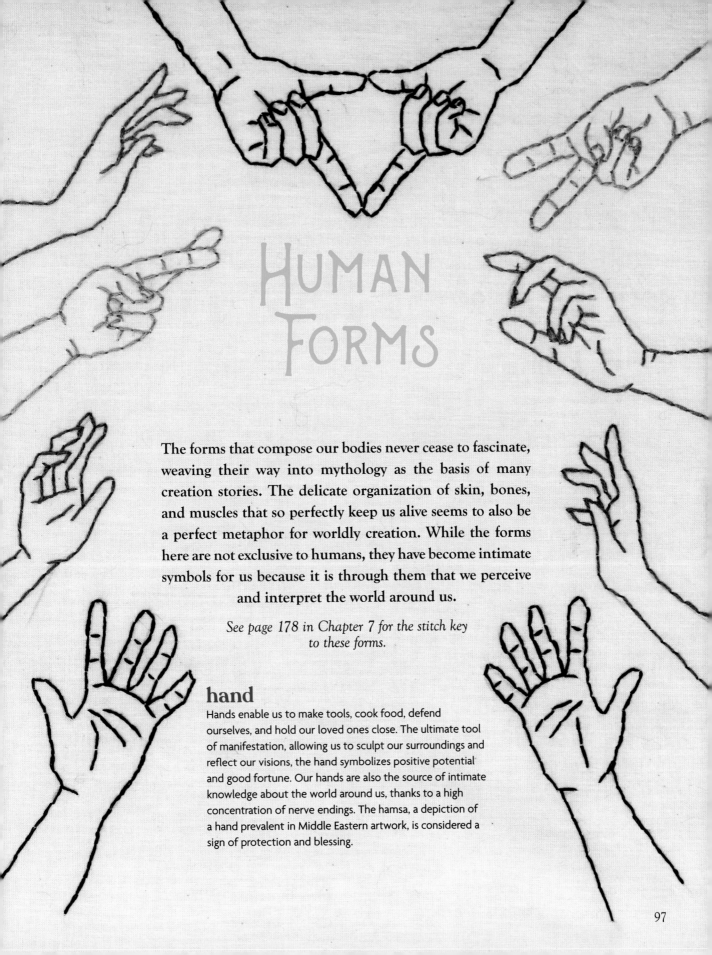

HUMAN FORMS

The forms that compose our bodies never cease to fascinate, weaving their way into mythology as the basis of many creation stories. The delicate organization of skin, bones, and muscles that so perfectly keep us alive seems to also be a perfect metaphor for worldly creation. While the forms here are not exclusive to humans, they have become intimate symbols for us because it is through them that we perceive and interpret the world around us.

See page 178 in Chapter 7 for the stitch key to these forms.

hand

Hands enable us to make tools, cook food, defend ourselves, and hold our loved ones close. The ultimate tool of manifestation, allowing us to sculpt our surroundings and reflect our visions, the hand symbolizes positive potential and good fortune. Our hands are also the source of intimate knowledge about the world around us, thanks to a high concentration of nerve endings. The hamsa, a depiction of a hand prevalent in Middle Eastern artwork, is considered a sign of protection and blessing.

eye

The space where we open up to receive the light of the cosmos, the eye symbolizes all-seeing, all-knowing wisdom, and enlightenment accessed through intuition. Incorporate its imagery as an invitation for clear-sighted guidance and trust in a greater vision.

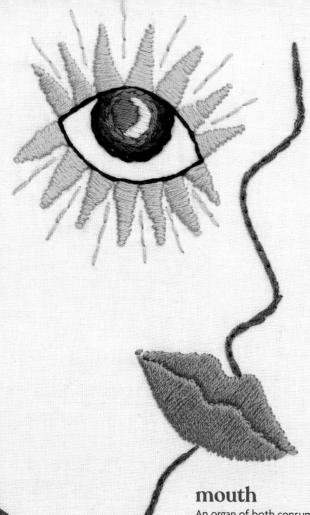

ear

With a shape suggesting the spiral shell form, the human ear collects waves of sound from which we gather information on our surroundings. The liquids in the labyrinth of tubes allow us to find our balance. In its relation to water and shells, the ear is receptive by nature, taking in and absorbing our surroundings in a most magical way.

mouth

An organ of both consumption and expression, the mouth generates words and communication. It offers an opportunity for intimacy through whispers and, of course, the kiss. Like love, the mouth devours and consumes and, through this action, keeps us vibrantly alive.

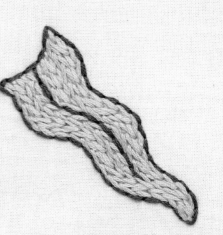

teeth

The hardest part of the human body, responsible for gripping and grinding food into digestible bits, our teeth symbolize our ability to assimilate outside substances, whether food or mental and spiritual concepts. A dream about the loss of teeth can be interpreted as the feeling of a loss of control or an inability to properly grip onto or predigest life situations.

tongue

Lending us the ability to distinguish flavors and to create the variety of sounds that compose language, the tongue possesses the capability of discernment. Perhaps due to its serpentlike shape, many Christian depictions of an extended tongue imply evil forces. In contrast, the Hindu goddess Kali is shown with her tongue extended, possibly as a symbol of the eventual consumption of all by the mouth of nature.

skull

The skull is a reminder of death and our transient nature, while also holding the notion that in death we are all equal. In artwork, the skull becomes an opportunity to meditate on death as a way to infuse your current existence with more meaning. The art form known as memento mori is Latin for "Remember that you will die." The skull is often the personification of death in many world mythologies, including Aztec, Hindu, Norse, and East Asian.

hair

A lock of hair would be given to a lover as a sign of devotion, taken from another in a quest for power, or saved as a memento of those who have passed. In loose tangles or neatly kept braids, deeply rich in color or sparkling with strands of silver, our hair is a closely held part of our personal identities.

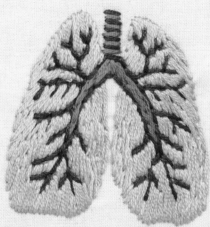

heart

This pulsing organ at the center of our physical form keeps its own life-sustaining beat. It has been shown that the heart sends more messages to the brain than the brain does to the heart. As we know certain things "in our core," it's as though they come directly from the heart. Work with this symbol to access your own inner-knowing and to tune in to the personal rhythms of your physical form.

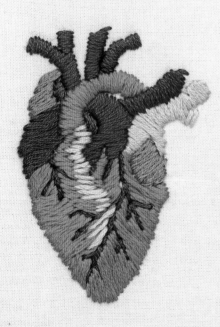

lungs

Another word for inhale is *inspire*. This act is only possible when we have properly exhaled and eliminated what is not needed, cleansing our system through breath. Breath work is an ancient technique for clearing out stagnancy in the body. A simple series of deep breaths in and out can do wonders for your system. Work with the symbol of the lungs as a sign of discernment and in support of clarity. Oh, and take a deep breath!

foot

While modern culture may depict feet as lowly or dirty forms, the bare foot's closeness to the earth is a sign of a grounding connection with nature itself, much like the humble and hardworking earthworm. The concept of keeping a "solid footing" and "grounding" yourself highlights the foot as a symbol of strengthening your personal roots in the world.

Our Tools

The forms of these mundane tools and objects hold symbolic importance for us beyond their functional uses. The tools here are enduring and universal; they show up in almost all ancient societies and continue to be of use in our modern world. They may take on slightly different visual styles, but their meanings draw parallels across cultures.

See page 180 in Chapter 7 for the stitch key to these forms.

candle

Able to illuminate a room with a single flame, the candle is a symbol of divinity, wisdom, and purification. However, its ability to be extinguished or burned down completely hints at the mortal nature of our existence.

vase

A container of divine waters, the vase is the symbolic womb, the place where the great mother holds the fertile waters of existence. Allow the vase to serve you as an ever-flowing source of nourishment. Feel free to stitch the surface of your vase with symbols that support this intention for you.

rope

Are you bound and tied, or is the rope a tool for accessing otherwise unavailable realms? In some cases, a tool's significance depends entirely on how we choose to view it.

wand

A simple branch holds within it the possibility to become a conduit of personal power when infused with supernatural forces. How will you choose to direct your power? In the tarot, the suit of wands is related to the element of fire, the flame of action, transformation, and potential.

wheel

Rolling in constant motion, the wheel asks us to accept the unceasing transformative reality of our existence. Can we find comfort within the unknown and impermanence? Everything is ephemeral. Used in Buddhism to display the eight paths of right living— while everything is moving, the center stays still.

comb

The act of combing implies sorting through and organizing the strands of chaos. With teeth that resemble the rays of the sun, this tool of discernment also symbolizes an opportunity for enlightenment. It is related to the loom in sorting out threads so they can be woven into the fabric of our lives.

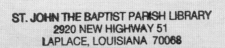

door

An initiation into the unknown, the door beckons you to enter new worlds. It is also an entirely functional protective passage into your home. The doorway holds many superstitions at its threshold; hanging herbs and sprinkled powders protect the home, and sacred symbols placed by the door invite abundance. Open doors are an opportunity for discovery and transcendence; a closed door serves to protect and keep safe.

key

Within such a small piece of metal lies access to great mysteries and deep knowledge. The key can be a source of liberation, if you are able to discover exactly where it fits. It holds the energy of initiation into as yet unknown dimensions.

stairs or ladder

Moving us through space, stairs and ladders are a method of communication between different levels of consciousness and the cosmos. They provide the means for both ascension and descension, an opportunity to connect with divinity or our own deep mysteries.

pyramid

The exact purpose of the pyramids remains unknown, enhancing their monumental mystery. With corners that land precisely on the four directions, and lines straighter than modern tools could create, the pyramid astounds and inspires. Its shape is thought to be an interpretation of the rays of the sun with the apex being the highest attainable knowledge and possibility.

bowl

This humble vessel is a sign of receptivity, a place to collect and gather that which we require. Allow the bowl to symbolize the benefits of sitting back and receiving. We don't always need to be outwardly active.

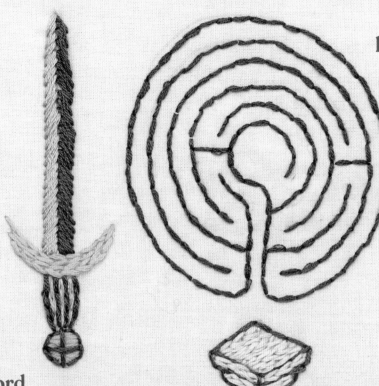

labyrinth

The winding paths to our centers are illustrated by the labyrinth. As we move to the center, we may lose our grip on which direction we are headed, disorienting our reality. This can allow us to transcend the rational perspective and access deeper spiritual knowledge.

broom

By cleansing and purifying a space, the broom sweeps out and banishes bad energy along with the dust and dirt. Historically associated with witches, it holds a deeper alignment with the expression of feminine power through daily acts in the domestic realm.

sword

Depending on which edge you choose, the sword can be a sign of decisiveness and strength of mind or a symbol of conflict. It represents the active intellect, whether in a peaceful or violent act. Do you choose creation or destruction? Is one possible without the other? In the tarot, it symbolizes the element of air, related to our thoughts and intellectual discrimination.

pillar

A quite literal symbol of stability and wisdom in its positioning in architecture, the pillar acts as a vertical axis from earth to heaven. Pillars often frame institutions of power and knowledge.

temple

The temple is an earthly manifestation of the palace for communing with the divine. The ascending stairs bring us up toward the cosmos, while the four corners keep us grounded in earthly realms. What does the space look like where your divinity dwells?

coin

A sign of abundance, value, and possibilities in the earthly realms, the coin can also serve as a reminder not to allow your values to focus too strongly on material gains. The suit of coins, also called pentacles, represents the element of earth in the tarot.

mask

A ritual storytelling tool, the mask gives us an opportunity to take on different forms and a place to hide from our societal roles. The mask holds its own power by simply transforming the wearer's appearance—or by transforming their persona entirely. Does the mask disguise your true nature or allow you to expose it for all to see?

chain

A visual representation of physical constraints, a chain can be broken (as in domination) or chosen (as in relationships). You can decide how you relate to chains that link or bind.

hourglass

A symbol of the transitory, the rushing sand in a curved hourglass reminds us of our finite existence.

chalice

This vessel of divine waters is often elaborately decorated. The chalice in religion symbolizes the search for a source to uplift the soul from worldly concerns into spiritual realms. In the tarot, cups represent the suit of water and our expressions of relationships to others, to ourselves, and to the deeper realms of our subconscious.

knot

A visual representation of connection and union—as in "tying the knot" of marriage—the eternal knot symbolizes continuity and integration. The knot also hints at what has us all tied up. Do you find yourself restrained by your own will or bound to certain situations by choice?

CREATING YOUR TALISMAN

Now it's time to take all your knowledge of stitches and symbolism, stir them into the cauldron, and cook up some magic! If you want to keep it simple, choose an image from the Treasury of Symbols (Chapter 4) to stitch onto a garment. I'll share a few of my own talismans, developed for specific intentions. If you want to get really creative, you can design your own composition through a combination of symbols. Inspired to choose your own talisman adventure? Let's dive in!

Color Harmony

The vibrations of light we've come to know as color are actually visual phenomena communicated to our brains by the inner workings of our eyes. A single color is entirely relative to the surrounding light and colors, and to the way it's absorbed in the eye of the beholder. Much like our personal relationships to symbols, color is a language with which we are able to go beyond words to express feelings and energies understood by the soul. This element of creativity is extremely personal—we all have our own distinct emotions and meanings tied to color—and it can help us clarify our intentions.

The Color Globe

There are no solid rules or final theory to this personal element of design, but a color globe might help you explore color options with a stronger base of knowledge. Just like your ability to cook can be enhanced by understanding the chemical reactions happening in the pot, your ability to create artwork is enhanced by understanding what colors are made up of. The color globe is not necessary—color knowledge can be intuitive, like cooking—but it will enable you to design embroidery without a pattern much faster, similar to cooking a meal without a recipe.

See the facing page for my model of the color globe. Imagine that you can climb inside of this three-dimensional globe—there are infinite colors within and you can take a slice out of it to see more nuanced options.

Hue

Hue is defined as pure color without any white, gray, or black added. If we travel around the surface of this globe from east to west, we see the colors change in hue. The equator is where you find pure color, without white or black. So if you're standing on pure yellow and you start walking along the equator, you'll find yourself traveling toward orange then red then purple and so on until you get back to yellow.

Value

Value is the change in lightness or darkness of a color. The center pole of the globe is shades of white, black, and gray. Traveling up and down this axis will allow you to find lighter or darker shades of color. At the north pole there are options for pastels. The south pole is black and surrounded by deep shades of color. The center core of the globe is a medium gray.

Saturation

Saturation is the change in the brightness or dullness of a color. If you travel into the globe toward the core, you'll find the colors go from full saturation—bright and vibrant on the surface—to dull as you near the gray center.

Warm, Cool, and Complementary

Colors described as warm (red, orange, yellow) are on one half of the globe, and cool colors (purple, blue, green) are on the other half. Colors that are complementary lie opposite one another on the globe. Thus, blue and orange are complementary colors. Green is complementary to red. Yellow is complementary to purple. This applies to the full range of hues—so an orangey-yellow sits opposite, and is complementary to, a bluish purple.

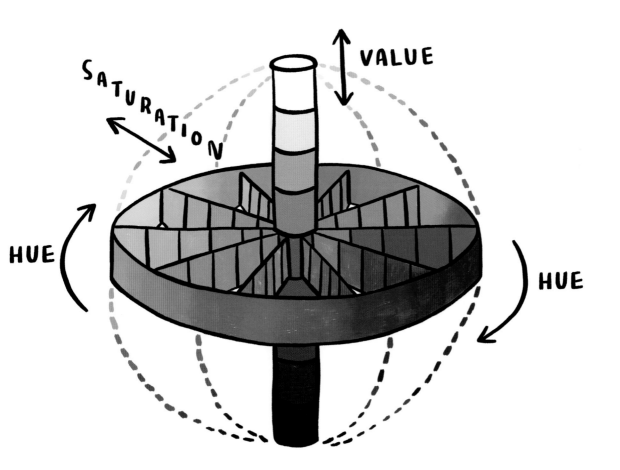

Choosing Colors

Color has enormous influence on your final artwork. Simply changing the hue of a design element or depth of shade can completely transform a piece of artwork. There are some traditional methods of learning and experiencing how different colors interact within a piece of work. These concepts are based on the color wheel, which is what you would see if you sliced the color globe across the equator and viewed the flat surface. The color wheel includes all hues but does not describe all levels of value and saturation.

* **Analogous colors** are shades that lie next to one another on the wheel (blue and green, for example). Using them together creates a soft flow that expresses harmony and a feeling of unity.

* **Monotone colors** are the same hue, in darker and lighter shades. For example, a deep green and a very light green. Using them together creates an effect that is calming yet richly dimensional. This is perfect for creating shadows within a piece of work.

* **Triadic color** is a selection of colors on the wheel that form an equilateral triangle (red, blue, and yellow, for example). These unexpected combinations create a lively and exciting contrast in color.

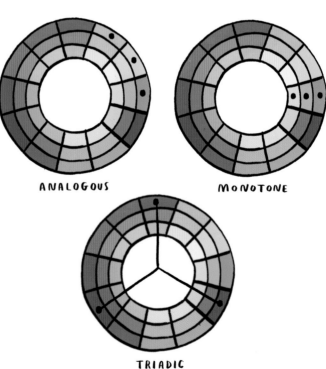

ANALOGOUS

MONOTONE

TRIADIC

* **Split complementary.** By combining the harmony of analogous colors with the excitement of complementary colors, the palette created with four shades of a split complementary selection is stimulating without being jarring.

* **Liminal space.** The places in between are the most beautiful. These are hard to clearly describe when looking at a color wheel. Colors like camel brown, dusty peach, and denim blue lie outside of the bold primary and secondary hues we are most familiar with. One of my favorite ways of choosing colors for a palette is to travel across the globe in an arc, so that the color is getting darker while it is also changing hue.

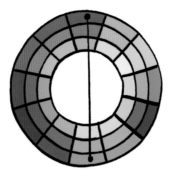

COMPLEMENTARY

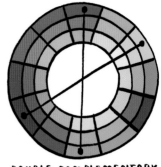

DOUBLE COMPLEMENTARY

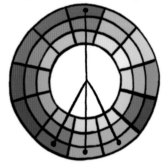

SPLIT COMPLEMENTARY

TIPS AND TRICKS

* Begin with a limited selection. Choosing about five colors allows you to have plenty of options while also providing a sense of harmony throughout the design, even within opposites.

* Don't place the entire skein on the fabric when selecting colors. Pull out a few inches of thread to look at against the fabric. Seeing how a single thread looks is much more valuable when deciding on your palette.

* Make sure there's contrast between the threads and the fabric. Test a few stitches and view them from a distance to be sure you can see the final piece of work.

Mystical Color

What we interpret as color is actually energy. Color is created through different vibrations of light hitting our retina, and the inner mechanics of our eyes then translate this information so our brain can map our surroundings. Each shade of the rainbow can influence our emotions, moods, and perceptions. While each person may respond to color differently, here are some associations that may help you choose hues for your artwork that reflect your desired intentions.

RED. An intense shade of passion, like the blood coursing through our veins and the molten core of our Earth, red roots us in the physical. Associated with the planet Mars, red can enhance romance and help you find willpower, though it can be a bit aggressive. This fiery hue can also assist in cutting ties with something that is no longer in your best interest.

ORANGE. A stimulating hue blending the activeness of red with the joyfulness of yellow, orange brings vibrant and playful energy. It can be applied to help release resistance to change, inspire new ideas, and open up communication. It is associated with the planet Mercury.

YELLOW. This bright hue associated with the sun channels our luminary star to help enhance focus and call upon abundance and joy. It is also considered the color of healing, as it stimulates the flow of energy in the body.

GREEN. A representation of growth and expansion, green brings harmony and facilitates a sense of community. Associated with Venus, this hue is an opportunity to connect to the feelings of love and abundance present in the natural world.

BLUE. This grounding hue can help us find clarity, assisting with communication in this world and with other dimensions in a way that is calming and peaceful. Related to the moon, blue can be incorporated when in need of accessing intuition and tapping into the unknown.

PURPLE. Finding guidance through spiritual energy, purple is a color of balance and beauty. It is frequently used in spiritual work. Associated with the planet Jupiter, purple can help you expand your connection to divine realms.

BROWN. Connecting us to the deep mysteries of compost and soil, brown is also related to the earth. It asks us to consider the growth that happens underground, not immediately visible yet still making all the difference in keeping us supported.

Exploring Composition

The key to creating your talisman is choosing symbols that correspond to the intention you wish to set, so you're sending your message out in a clear and condensed collection of images. By organizing the symbols in a way that amplifies their essence, you can make your composition as expressive as the symbols themselves.

To create your own talisman, use a combination of symbols and arrange them in visually pleasing and energetically amplifying ways. You can use composition and scale to emphasize your intention.

Begin by choosing symbols that speak to you, and write down an intention that ties these images together and describes their purpose. This will come in handy later. There's nothing more exciting and gratifying than looking back on your intentions and realizing how beautifully they manifested.

Don't know which symbols to combine? Here's a recipe: Choose one primary symbol, a supporting botanical, and another supporting symbol that can be stitched small and serve as an activator in multiples—for example, five stars to enhance spiritual growth, three circles to support unity, or four arrows for stability in action. Make copies of the symbols and play around with the layout by pinning them on your fabric. This can help you visualize the finished results.

If you're overwhelmed by options or not convinced you love your design, walk away for a bit. Take some deep breaths, go for a stroll, pet a cat or dog, talk to a bird, sit under a tree. A change of scenery can help you return to the work with more clarity. Whatever you do, don't force it. Sometimes ideas are stubborn or just not ready to be born yet.

Compositions with elements of different sizes allow energy to move more freely.

A radial composition—where things are arranged like rays coming out of a center point—emphasizes the central symbol, while the surrounding elements play a supporting role.

A classic wreath style is a great way for your supporting herbs to shine.

Transcendent Talisman

You can combine symbols from the Treasury in Chapter 4 to design your own talisman. The following are a few I've created for specific intentions. Choose one that speaks strongly to you and create an embroidery piece to put on your altar, stitch onto clothing, or adorn your pillowcase. Put it someplace where you will encounter it frequently to remind you of your intentions for personal evolution. See page 183 for the stitch key to these projects.

Ouroboros of Transformation

A symbol of our cyclical nature and infinite possibilities for renewal, the snake devouring its own tail is known as an ouroboros. The flame of transformation swiftly engulfs the ways of the past, burning them off in order to bring about new potential. This is a talisman for embracing change and aligning yourself with your true powers.

See the pattern on page 184.

1. Outline the snake in silver, using blanket stitch for the belly side and backstitch for the outer edge and head.

2. Use silver to create Xs of snake scales by filling the outer edge of the body with diagonal stitches in one direction, beginning at the spokes of the blanket stitch. Then cross over these with diagonal stitches in the other direction.

3. Beginning at the inside of the fire, chain stitch single rows of copper. Surround these with a row of golden chain stitch at the top. Finish the flames by surrounding in yellow chain stitch.

4. Add stars in ivory using French knots and star stitch. Add the snake eyes in ivory by making two detached chain stitches next to one another; top with a French knot in copper.

5. Create crosses in copper at the bottom with straight stitches tacked down at their intersection. Then make French knot dots surrounding the snake at top.

Serpent, page 80
Stars, page 57
Cross, page 58

SCARAB OF ABUNDANCE

Two glistening golden coins serve as wings to lift this sun-worshipping winged one toward a bright and prosperous future. The scarab's hard exterior is emblazoned with climbing vines as a sign of growth and abundance. This is a prosperity talisman created to draw bountiful earthly pleasures.

See the pattern on page 185.

1. Stitch the vines on the scarab's wing covers in teal, using satin stitch for the leaves and stem stitch for the stem. Fill in the remainder of the wing covers and the face of the coins with yellow using long and short stitch.

2. Fill in the diamond on the scarab's upper back in ivory using satin stitch, then stem stitch stripes out to its edge.

3. Create rays beneath the coins using ray stitch in ivory. Then make two stars with ivory, using straight stitch, on each side of the scarab.

4. Chain stitch the star at the top.

5. Fill in the scarab's head with olive using long and short stitch; then outline the scarab and the coins with three strands of dark brown.

6. Fill in the remainder of the body with dark brown satin stitch.

7. Finally, create stripes on the coins with yellow and dark brown in alternating straight stitches.

Scarab, page 80
Coins, page 104
Stars, page 57

PORTALS TO THE UNKNOWNS

Above a glistening sea, a doorway emerges flanked by rich olive-green grasses and the ever-changing cycles of the moon. We know not what the star in the opening promises, but we're beckoned to find out. This talisman encourages personal expansion through taking a step into the unknown.

See the pattern on page 186.

1. Stitch the doorway using satin stitch in alternating blocks of pale gold and lavender. Create dots around the door in pale gold using French knots.

2. Chain stitch waves in pale blue, adding stars to the top with star stitch.

3. With olive, create blades of grass using stem stitch.

4. Finish up with satin-stitched moons in ivory; then use satin stitch for each arm of the star inside the door.

5. To hide areas where these satin stitches meet, overlap with a star stitch; the end of each spoke of the star stitch will line up with the inner corners of the satin-stitched star.

Door, page 102
Waves, page 58
Moon, page 70
Stars, page 57

LOVE FLOWS FREELY

A golden chalice rises from a blooming lotus. The waters of our emotional realm flow from the chalice without blockage, nourishing the earth with the gift of our passion fully expressed. This is a talisman for assistance in relaxing enough to fully feel your emotions.

See the pattern on page 187.

1. Satin stitch the stem of the chalice with brown. Form the sides of the chalice with long and short stitch. Using long and short stitch, fill in the chalice with copper toward the middle and yellow in the center.

2. With chain stitch alternating in navy and pale blue, stitch waves of flowing water. Stitch droplets at the top in pale blue with diagonal satin stitch.

3. In dusty rose, create a lotus flower at the bottom with diagonal satin stitch and coral at the sides with feather stitch.

Chalice, page 105
Waves, page 58
Droplets, page 95
Lotus, page 92
Coral, page 77

THE HEART THAT GROWS

Rosemary rises up from a heart-shaped vessel. As its roots grow deeper, this herb reminds you of where you came from while the shimmering eye keeps a vision toward your biggest dreams. This is a talisman created for connecting to the deepest, most expansive truths of your heart with your desired future.

See the pattern on page 188.

1. In dark red, stitch roots at the bottom of the heart/vase with backstitch and straight stitch.

2. Using long and short stitch, fill in the heart starting at the outside with dark red, followed by red toward the middle and to fill in the neck. Then fill in all but the eye in dusty red.

3. Backstitch the outline of the heart and the eye in black. Fill in the middle of the eye with satin stitch in black.

4. Stem stitch herbs at the top in olive green, and satin stitch rays in yellow.

5. Using two rows of chain stitch close together, fill in the iris of the eye in blue.

Root, page 87
Heart, page 99
Vase, page 101
Eye, page 98
Rosemary, page 89

Enliven Your Closet

Our clothes are our second skin. We may take them for granted sometimes, but they serve many purposes, from protection to expression, and they are one of our most important physical possessions. To stitch a talisman into a piece of clothing is to infuse your daily threads with your highest intentions for your life, while also delightfully decorating your wardrobe. Allow your stitches to breathe new life—and meaning—into your garments.

When you're stitching onto a garment, work on a part that rests on the flat planes of the body—the front or back of the shoulder, the outside of the biceps, the outside of a pant leg, and wherever pockets are located. This will make for a more aesthetically pleasing result because these areas aren't at risk of bunching up and the images won't be distorted during wear. Avoid concentrated stitching on thick seams, especially in denim. Also, embroidery in areas that are highly voluminous, like the pleated or gathered area at the waistline of a skirt, tends to get lost.

Tips for Working on Garments

* Some areas of button-down shirts, especially the edges, are difficult to stitch with an embroidery hoop. For these areas, you'll want to keep stitches a little looser than normal to avoid puckering. If you feel the need to hold the fabric taut, there are a few little tricks I like to use: One is to hold an edge of the garment in between my knees, pulling slightly with the hand that holds the fabric. Another is to actually pin the garment to my jeans to create tension while I sew, which is a little less of a thigh workout than the previous technique. Just be sure not to sew your project to your own clothes!

* Stitching on a collar, placket, or other areas where the fabric is doubled looks best (and the garment lies best) when only the surface fabric is embroidered. In doing this, you also hide the underside of the stitches between the two layers of fabric. With your hand on the back of the fabric, you can feel when you've inserted the needle too far.

* For these collar or placket areas where the fabric is doubled, you can use a hidden knot trick to hide your threads. Instead of pulling from the back to the front, try hiding the tail of your thread in between the two layers of fabric. Pull the needle through from an inch or so away from where your stitching will begin (preferably at the edge of a seam) with the needle traveling in between the two layers of fabric to hide this tail of thread. Then exit in an area where you can make two tiny stitches that will blend into the rest of the embroidery (see the knot-on-fabric technique, page 27). Cut off any remaining thread tail close to the fabric when done. Repeat this process when you're finished with a length of thread, creating two tiny stitches to secure the thread before sending the needle through the layers an inch or so

away from this hidden knot. Cut the remaining thread close enough to the fabric so that it disappears.

✳ It is way too easy to stitch a pocket shut when adding embroidery to it! I usually stick my hand in the pocket both to hold the fabric taut and to be sure I'm not sewing through both layers—double win!

✳ Stitching on cuffs looks really great, but before you begin, consider whether you tend to roll the sleeves up when wearing the shirt. This may seem obvious, but too many times I've made the mistake of embroidering an area that ends up hidden!

✳ Always try on the clothing after you've transferred the design onto it. Think of it like this: When you get a tattoo, you want to look at the drawing on your skin in the mirror before the tattoo artist gets to work. It may take a little more time; you may even have to erase and redraw the transfer, but it's better than having a tattoo you wish had been just a little smaller and to the right (like, for example, the rushed tattoo on my forearm).

✳ The front buttonhole placket is a great place to add embroidery, but many shirts are worn open in a way that this stitching might not be seen. Be sure to try on the shirt and see how the placket lies before stitching on it. I usually don't stitch between the collar and the first or second buttonhole for this reason.

Amulet Adornment Necklace

This will help keep your intentions close to your heart as you travel. Choose dried herbs that correspond to your wishes, and include a small quartz or another crystal to help amplify the positive qualities you've infused into your stitches.

For this project, you will embroider your design on the fabric (directions here) and then make the necklace (page 132).

1. Fill in the waves in ivory using two rows of chain stitch for the two larger waves, and a single row of chain stitch for the small wave's tapering ends of chain stitch.

2. Use backstitch to outline the waves in brown.

3. Add accents of star stitch and French knots in yellow.

CRYSTALS AND HERBS FOR FILLING
Stuff your amulet with quartz and lavender for cleansing and clearing energy. For support in love, use garnet or rose quartz with lemon balm, rose, or yarrow. To bring abundance, try citrine with goldenrod or calendula.

Waves, page 58
Stars, page 57

MAKING AN AMULET NECKLACE

FABRIC SIZE: 2 inches wide* × 6 inches long if using a 4-inch hoop; longer if using a larger hoop

FINISHED SIZE: 1½ inches wide × 2 inches tall

*If using a heavier fabric, allow ⅜ inch for seam allowance instead of ¼ inch and cut the fabric 2¼ inches wide.

1. Mark the fabric at the seam allowances and the midpoint, which will be the top of the necklace. Mark the fabric 2 inches from the midpoint, which will be the bottom of the necklace. Draw your design.

2. Secure the fabric in the hoop and embroider your design. Cut to the finished length after you're done embroidering, adding seam allowance at both ends. Press under the seam allowance at the sides.

3. Measure out 64 inches each of the three colors of embroidery floss. Holding the three together, fold them in half and knot the folded end. Create rope by braiding the three colors together using doubled threads. Knot again at the finished end.

4. Place the knotted ends of the rope at each side of the midpoint mark. Fold the fabric with wrong sides together and pin so that the knots are held securely inside.

5. Using a tiny whip stitch about ⅛ inch long, sew up the outer edges, being sure to securely stitch down the braided rope at the top corners. Leave the bottom edge open for stuffing.

6. Gently fill with herbs and stones until about three-quarters full. You don't need it totally stuffed. Fold the seam allowance at the bottom edge inward; then sew up the bottom edge with a whip stitch.

7. Cut six strands of embroidery floss at 6 inches long. Thread a needle with about 10 inches of matching floss and insert the needle through the bottom corner of the amulet. Pull the thread through halfway so you have two 5-inch strands coming off of the bottom corner.

8. Tie these two ends around the middle of the six strands, then gather all the strands, except one of the long ends, together to form your tassel. With the remaining long end, wrap around (about ¼ inch down from the top of the tassel) a few times to bind the top of the tassel.

9. Tie a knot around this wrapped area and use a needle to pull the loose end up through the top of the tassel and through the corner of the amulet, so the loose end of the thread is buried inside the amulet. Trim ends evenly. Repeat on other side.

GALACTIC DENIM JEANS

Give your jeans a design that is out of this world. This pattern keeps you in tune with the vastness of the cosmos.

See the pattern on page 189.

1. Beginning with the pale gold thread, use a detached chain stitch for the large star and satin stitch for the moon.

2. Continue down the leg, stitching the cosmic stardust with star stitch and French knots. If there's more than 1 inch between motifs, knot the thread at the back of the fabric at the end of one motif, cut it, tie another knot, and restart. This keeps the threads on the back neat, and you're less likely to snag the stitches when pulling your jeans on.

3. The curvy lines of the galactic mist begin with French knots or running stitch, then thicken into stem stitch, thinning out again with French knots or running stitch.

4. Stitch the remaining cosmic stardust in ivory, mint, and dark green.

5. Using the long and short satin stitch technique, fill in the top and bottom of the planet in mint green. The ring is created using a chain stitch in copper, then outlined with backstitch in dark green.

6. For the snake, begin with the dark green line at the center, using stem to satin stitch to create a thicker line in the area of the head. Return to a regular stem stitch down through the middle of the body.

7. In pale gold thread, outline the central green line of the snake using stem stitch. Be sure all the stitches on the snake are the same angle (see the S and Z rule in the stem stitch instructions, page 35). Stop the pale gold 1 inch before the end of the snake to taper the tail.

8. With copper thread, repeat what you stitched in pale gold. Stop another ½ inch up the body to taper the tail.

9. Finish the snake with a mint-green outline. Use stem to satin stitch to thicken at the head, as you did with the dark green stitch at the beginning.

Stars, page 57
Moon, page 70
Planets, page 67
Serpent, page 80

FIFTH POCKET PORTAL

This little portal reminds us of the opportunities available in even the smallest of places. This project is a joy to watch take shape.

1. Measure the opening of the fifth pocket from the innermost stitch line to the opposite innermost stitch line, and divide this by 7. No need to be super precise here; this is not a math test. If measuring in inches is complicated, try the metric system, which divides nicely when using small quantities (6 cm equals 60 mm, and 60 divided by 7 equals 8.5 mm). Or just eyeball it!

2. Using the number you came up with, mark seven equally spaced areas across the pocket between the stitch lines. I promise no one will notice if you're a millimeter or two off! Now, using the same width (8.5 mm in our example), mark three horizontal stripes to complete the square shapes in each color.

3. Draw a diagonal line from the top outer corners to the top corners of the innermost stripe.

4. Using the brown thread, and bringing the needle from the bottom outer edge of the fifth pocket up to the front, satin stitch the outer stripe. Shorten up your stitches along the diagonal line as you near the corner. Use your fingers inside the pocket to keep the fabric taut and prevent stitching the pocket closed. When you get to the corners where a diagonal line is drawn, continue with satin stitch but end your stitches on the diagonal line. This means your stitches will get consecutively shorter as they get closer to the corner.

5. With the gold thread, start at the bottom as before and satin stitch the second stripe.

6. Repeat with the remaining stripes. If you run out of thread and are having a hard time knotting inside the pocket (in some areas this is nearly impossible), use the knot-on-fabric method (page 27).

Step 1

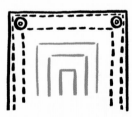

Step 2

Step 3

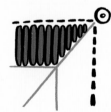

Step 4

Visionary Denim Shirt

Providing you with the ability to see in all directions, this visionary pattern is perfect for the back shoulders of your favorite denim shirt.

See the pattern on page 190.

1. Find the center of the yoke (the upper back of the shirt) by folding the shirt in half and lining up the shoulder seams. Mark the fold with pins or a removable marking tool.

2. Outline the eye with a navy-blue chain stitch, and fill in the first section of each ray with the same. Taper the ends by tacking down the last chain stitch with a long stitch. Then begin the journey back to the edge of the eye with a chain stitch that starts about three-quarters of the way down (see chain stitch instructions on page 41 for how to create points).

3. Again using navy floss, start at the outer edge and fill in the iris with four rows of chain stitch close together.

4. With ivory thread, fill in the outer whites of the eye with chain stitch, starting at the outside and filling in with stitches close together.

5. Use chain or satin stitch to fill in the tiny circle in the middle of the eye.

6. With cobalt, outline each of the outer rays. Be sure to extend the ends a few stitches beyond the navy rays, and taper the points by using a long stitch to tack down the last chain stitch.

7. Continue with bright blue, filling in any gaps between your stitches with stem stitch to be sure the points stay nice and straight. Repeat with light blue and ivory.

Eye, page 98

FORTUNE'S CONJURE JACKET

Origin of our ability to manifest, the hand is paired here with the sword of swift decision and the bay laurel branch of victory to call upon whatever it is we'd like to conjure for ourselves. This is a more time-consuming pattern, but it can be completed by stitchers of any skill level.

See the pattern on page 191.

1. If your jacket has a lining, open it up at the back seam or side seam using a seam ripper. You will only stitch through the outer layer of the fabric, leaving the lining loose. This will help hide the back of the embroidery. Just be sure to work in between the two layers by inserting your bottom hand into the seam of the lining you've opened so you don't end up sewing the lining to the back.

2. Find the center of the back by folding the jacket in half and lining up the shoulder seams and side seams. Mark this fold with pins or a removable marking tool, then transfer the pattern.

3. Using a diagonal satin stitch, fill in the bay laurel leaves in sage green and olive green.

4. Fill in the lightning bolts in golden yellow using satin stitch.

5. Fill in the blade of the sword with two shades of gray using satin stitch. Use two rows of chain stitch in dark gray for the handle of the sword, and outline with light gray in backstitch. Using two rows of chain stitch in golden yellow, fill in the guard of the handle on the sword, and finish the base of the handle with satin stitch in this same golden yellow.

6. Fill in the pyramids with satin stitch in gold and golden yellow, using long and short stitches for the larger area at the base.

7. Outline the hand with chain stitch in pale yellow. Backstitch the details on the inside of palm in this same pale yellow.

8. Each spoke of the star on top is created with chain stitches in pale yellow, all meeting in the middle. Create rays surrounding this star with three stem stitches per ray.

9. With dark brown, surround the outline of the hand in stem stitch, then add a stem and shadows to the bay laurel with stem stitch.

10. Outline the pyramids and details on the sword with backstitch in dark brown.

11. Use a small whip stitch to close up the opening in the lining.

6

The Art of Ritual

A magical act is performed with the goal of bringing about change in your life for the betterment of all. What distinguishes a magical act from a mundane act is not the physical objects used or even the exact motions made. Rather, an act is made magical through the intention you set. This intention can be amplified through a ritual. Religions and societies throughout time have developed specific rituals that require precise actions and materials, but those of us outside a traditional lineage seeking a personal connection with divine energies can develop our own rituals. While some traditions might have you think that only the holiest of holy can perform a ritual, there is actually no wrong way to create a ritual. From a mystical perspective, we are all capable of communing with divine forces. The divine already exists within us.

Setting Your Intention

When bringing ritual to your embroidered creations, you can create your talisman and then use a ritual to charge it; or you can make the act of creating the talisman a ritual itself. If you know you'll be stitching your talisman on the subway, it might not be ideal to develop an artistic ritual around this, so you may want to plan on charging your talisman in a ritual after the creation process. There is no one way to work magic or to make stitches—both are entirely personal experiences. This chapter offers some ideas to get your creativity ignited. First up: setting your intention.

✳ You'll want to begin your ritual with a reason for being, an intention you wish to manifest in the world, with harm to none. I add "with harm to none" as a reminder that ethics are of great importance when working magic!

✳ An intention works best as a single statement, and using alliteration or rhyming can be a fun way to infuse your words with a little enchantment. For example, if you're looking to move to a new home, you might chant, "An enchanting home so fine will soon enough be mine."

- The dual meaning of the word *spell* is no accident. To craft a spell in the magical sense is to string together a series of words that, when spoken aloud, amplify the effects of your work.

- Think of your intention as words of empowerment and a portal to new possibilities. While a clearly defined intention is great, leaving room for a boost from divine forces makes this collaboration more exciting.

- Once you've set an intention, spend a bit of time visualizing the transformations you desire as if they've already taken place. How does this new element of your life look fully manifested? How does it feel? What or whom are you surrounded by? What smells are traveling through the air? Having a vibrant and inspired image to return to gives your intention a little extra spark! Pay attention to any internal resistance you may have; bringing these doubts to the surface and facing them can help you move past them.

Building an Altar

Your altar is the home of your magical work. It is a sacred space you create to connect to higher powers—those within you and those in nature and the cosmos. By gathering together symbolic items in combination with your own energies, you create a well-balanced energetic container for your ritual. Including the five elements of nature (air, fire, water, earth, spirit) offers an opportunity to align your intentions with the energies of nature. You can use different objects, materials, mental images, and physical acts as symbols of the elements.

Air

Feathers, bells, smoke. Imagine the feeling of wind whipping by your face; notice the qualities of the air touching your skin; focus on and deepen the breath.

Fire

Candles, incense. Imagine the sensation of warmth and the crackling sounds of sitting in front of a bonfire; feel the heat in the core of your body radiating out as a bright flame.

Water

Seashells, coral, a small vial of water from a special place in nature. Allow your body to flow like water, gently swaying with the waves; or actually drink water.

ELEMENTAL INCENSE

Want a simple way to represent all five elements? Herbal incense burning in a seashell combines these beautifully. Incense represents earth, the shell represents water, lighting the incense represents fire, the smoke represents air, and the rising smoke is the essence of spirit. You can also add materials that call upon the planetary energies you wish to include (see Planetary Magic on page 67 for these cosmic archetypes) or any other associations you'd like to enhance your intentions.

Earth

Salt, dirt, rocks, herbs, house-plants. Imagine growing roots into the ground, lying on the ground, and feeling the weight of your body on the earth.

Spirit

Mandalas, stars, crystals, favored deities. Bring your awareness to the vast nature of the cosmos, the trillions of cosmic bodies burning alongside ours, and the tiniest microorganisms inhabiting the space with us.

Preparing for Ritual

Begin by cleansing your space in whatever way feels appropriate—with a broom, damp cloth, smoke, or even visualized light. Then declare this space as sacred. There are many options for defining your sacred space. One is to create a circle around you with your fingertip or a wand. Start from the east (air) and proceed to south (fire) to west (water) to north (earth) and back to the east. This method of creating sacred space can be found throughout history and across the globe.

Charging Your Talisman

The energy infused into a piece of work combined with the visual symbols you've chosen turns your stitched object into a talisman. To charge your talisman with personal empowerment, first give it an energetic cleansing by passing it through or fanning it with the smoke of incense. Then hold the embroidery between the palms of your hands, feeling the energies running through it—your energies of transformation, the earth's energies of regeneration, and any divine cosmic energies you choose to incorporate.

Feel these energies expanding outward, reaching to fill the sacred space you've defined. Recall your visualization of the forces you wish to call in. Now read your intention aloud with conviction and certainty to solidify the energy of empowerment. The most important element here is concentrating your mental energy on the visualization of the desired intention.

If you choose to make the act of stitching part of your ritual, try to hold this intention in your mind as you work.

⁂ While you're stitching, imagine the act of traveling between realms; see the symbols you're stitching being pulled up from your subconscious.

⁂ Allow the act of embroidery to slow you down and show you what you've been too rushed to see.

⁂ Allow the disparate elements of yourself—your external desires and your internal blocks—to be brought to the surface.

⁂ Visualize your intentions traveling down with the needle as it passes to the underside of the fabric and up again.

You have now charged your talisman with your intentions; while this may not override the negative aspects of our human experience, it might help you open up to new ways of living and new experiences you did not feel open to previously. Allow your talisman to act as your anchor—as a symbol of your power to create change in your life.

Closing Your Space

When your talisman is finished and you feel you've fully expressed your desires and any withheld aspects of self, uniting that which rises above and that which sits below the surface, take a few moments to integrate the conscious and the subconscious. Give thanks to all elements for their power in healing. Take a few deep breaths. Close up by retracing your circle, clapping your hands, doing a jig if you want, and reciting aloud "And so it is!"

Developing Your Creative Ritual

There are infinite ways to build the house of your creative actions. Coming from a place deep within, the ritual of a creative process does not require anything other than your focus and intention. Meditation, deep breathing, and physical movement cost nothing and can often do more to deepen your artistic ritual than the finest crystals, candles, or altar cloths.

You don't need anything more than a needle, some thread, and some free time to develop an artistic ritual for yourself. Sometimes I just curl up on the couch and the only preparation I do before I get to stitching is envisioning light expanding out and creating a sphere surrounding the space I'm working in. Other times, I like to light candles and arrange seashells, rocks,

feathers, and roots to create an elaborate scene around my artistic materials and support my process.

Your ritual might be something in between these two approaches; it all comes down to what works for you. Don't try to incorporate so many elements that your creative ritual turns into an over-whelming preparatory process that blocks you from getting started. It's perfectly fine to show up with only the power of your mind, strength in your convictions, and an appreciation for all that is. Ritual need not be complicated. Working with a few special objects can help with focus and dedicating this time as sacred; chanting your intention mentally can be one of the strongest tools.

Ritual in a Bag

The key to making a ritual into a regular habit is to make it easy and make it work with your life. I find it most effective to have all my supplies in one place and in a container that I enjoy looking at and has meaning for me. I have a small embroi-dered bag that I got many years ago on a trip to China. Its vibrant colors and hand-made details make it joyful to look at, even after all these years.

Inside the bag is a tiny pair of scissors, a wooden vial to hold needles, embroidery

floss in a broad selection of colors, a small embroidery hoop, and some folded-up fabric in black, white, and chambray blue. By keeping everything I need to embroider in this bag, I can easily take 20 to 30 min-utes to make a few stitches without having to gather all my supplies every time. I also love looking at this bag, so when I keep it on my desk, I'm more likely to remember to take time for some creative exploration.

Be Kind to Your Body

Any focused activity performed while seated can be hard on the body, especially on the neck and shoulders. Coordinating gentle stretches and deep breathing helps ease tension in the body as well as the mind. I frequently do a few yoga-inspired stretches while embroidering. Give yourself a break and play with the following suggestions. And be gentle with yourself. Consider these as warming stretches; your muscles are most likely cold and you should not push yourself, just gracefully engage these poses.

Cat Cow

On your hands and knees in a tabletop position, center your shoulders over your wrists, and your hips over your knees. As you inhale, gently lift your head and allow your belly to drop down. As you exhale, tuck your head and round your back, lifting your spine up toward the sky. Repeat for as long as feels necessary.

Standing Forward Bend

Standing straight and tall with your feet hip-distance apart, interlace your fingers behind your back, palms facing each other. Pull your hands downward, stretching your front shoulders open. Lengthen through the spine and, while keeping your back straight, gently bend forward from your hips on an exhale. Bend your legs a bit if you need to, and be sure not to lock your knees. Dangle your head in front of your legs with your arms behind you, allowing gravity to pull down on your arms just enough to feel a stretch.

Shoulder Circles

Sit cross-legged on the floor or a pillow and grasp your shoulders with your hands, fingers facing forward. Imagine drawing circles with your elbows, rotating at the shoulders, inhaling as your arms move up, exhaling as they move down.

Side Stretches

Sit cross-legged on the floor or a pillow. Reach your left arm high in the air on an inhale, and on an exhale gently reach your arm over your head and lean to the right just a bit, engaging your core to help keep your balance. Inhale back up straight; exhale down. Repeat on the other side.

Reclining Bound Angle

Known as Supta Baddha Konasana in yoga, this pose is one I like to enter at the close of any work I'm doing as a marker that the work is over. Lie on your back with your arms out to your sides. With knees bent and feet on the ground, open up your knees and allow the bottoms of your feet to come together. Use pillows to support your knees if needed. Breathe deeply, feel the stretch in your inner legs, and feel your chest open up gently.

CHAIN

RUNNING

STEM

the stitches

SATIN

BACK

STAR

FRENCH KNOT

BLANKET

STITCH KEY

Here are stitch instructions and patterns for the Treasury of Symbols (Chapter 4) so you can re-create them. You can combine symbols in a talisman or use them as a launch pad for your own creative designs. The numbers correspond to the colors of DMC embroidery floss I used. When I indicate "three-strand," that means splitting the six-strand embroidery floss in half. To download traceable patterns for all the symbols and projects in this book, visit www.storey.com/symbol-patterns/.

KEY TO STITCH TYPES

straight stitch	—·—·—·—·—·—
backstitch	— — — — — — —
split stitch	————————
stem stitch	/////////////////////
running stitch	— — — — — —
chain stitch	●●●●●●●●●●●●●●
wrapped chain stitch	～～～～～～～～
detached chain stitch	◇◇◇◇◇◇◇◇◇
fly stitch	﹥﹥﹥﹥﹥﹥﹥﹥﹥﹥﹥
feather stitch	﹥﹥﹥﹥﹥﹥﹥﹥﹥
blanket stitch	⊔⊔⊔⊔⊔⊔⊔⊔⊔⊔
French knots	∴
herringbone stitch	∧∧∧∧∧∧∧∧∧

seed stitch	
ray stitch	
star stitch	✳
satin stitch	
long and short stitch	
stem to satin stitch	

Geometric Forms

See Chapter 4, page 56, for symbols.

 **zigzag**
chain stitch with French knot
details (731, 720)

 STARS

all in 791, 720, 832, 823

    five points
from left: detached chain stitch; backstitch;
satin stitch; straight stitch

    six points
from left: star stitch; backstitch; satin stitch;
detached chain stitch, with short stitches
of contrast color on top

    seven points
from left: straight stitch; detached chain
stitch; backstitch; straight stitch

    eight points
from left: split stitch; satin stitch at a
diagonal; backstitch; star stitch

 half circle
French knots (646)

 square
satin stitch, alternating
colors (3799, 645)

 circle
satin stitch, alternating
colors (791, 680)

cross
satin stitch, with backstitch on top (798, 712)

wave
stem stitch (646)

arrow
backstitch (791)

triangle
seed stitch (3799)

spiral
stem stitch (798)

double helix
three-strand chain stitch outer spirals; backstitch inner stripes (830, 680, 798)

hut
Large: chain stitch; backstitch at bottom; satin stitch details. *Small:* backstitch (823, 680)

mandorla
starting from middle, four rows of three-strand chain stitch in consecutive colors to fill interior; straight stitch rays; running stitch outside (677, 728, 680, 830)

lozenge
satin stitch each row, starting at center (680, 975, 791, 823)

chevron
fly stitch (798, 823)

checkerboard
satin stitch (791, 798)

yin yang
three-strand chain stitch and French knot (310)

net
blanket stitch (823)

ankh
three-strand chain stitch, starting with lightest color on inside; backstitch rays (677, 3852, 830)

merkaba
long and short stitch; satin stitch
(3799, 645, 647, 648)

philosopher's stone
three-strand backstitch (830)

triskelion
three-strand chain stitch (310)

infinity
wrapped chain stitch (310, 648)

flower of life
Work out from center. Chain
stitch inner star, surrounding with
satin stitch on outer circles (677,
3852, 830, 333)

triple goddess
Work out from center. Chain stitch interior of middle
moon with five rows of lightest color; chain stitch
moons on side with one row; surround these lines
with next shade darker: one row of chain stitch
on middle moon, one row of stem stitch on outer
moons; repeat with next darkest color; stem stitch
border of all three moons with darkest color (341, 340,
333, 791)

Platonic Solids

All embroidery floss is split to three strands; outline in chain stitch with different stitched shading.

See Chapter 4, page 62, for symbols.

dodecahedron
shading in French knots (340)

tetrahedron
shading in chain stitch (930)

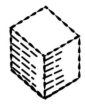

cube
shading in backstitch (975)

octahedron
shading in running stitch (844)

icosahedron
shading in seed stitch (830)

Numbers

See Chapter 4, page 64, for symbols.

0
chain stitch to outline, then fill in with chain stitch; top with star stitch, satin stitch, and French knots (310, 3817)

1
three rows of chain stitch, starting from inner row; satin stitch lightning (720, 561, 3817, 3852)

2
backstitch (310, 918)

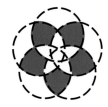
3
backstitch; satin stitch inside (918, 720)

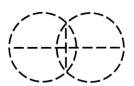
4
satin stitch interior triangles and exterior stripe; chain stitch gold diamond stripe; three-strand backstitch around chain stitch; three-strand French knots in outer corners (561, 3817, 3852, 310)

5
backstitch outline; fill in with satin stitch (823, 720)

6
satin stitch interior triangle; three-strand backstitch surrounding rows (832, 798, 3752)

7
satin stitch interior stars; French knot surrounding (823, 798, 3752)

8
chain stitch interior star; straight stitch surrounding stripes (720, 798)

9
backstitch triangular shapes and interior stripes; satin stitch interior circles; straight stitch rays on outside (823, 832, 720)

Planetary Magic

Saturn, Jupiter, and Uranus are stitched in chain stitch. All other planets are stitched using satin stitch and long and short stitch. Planetary symbols are backstitch, and orbits are running stitch.

See Chapter 4, page 67, for symbols.

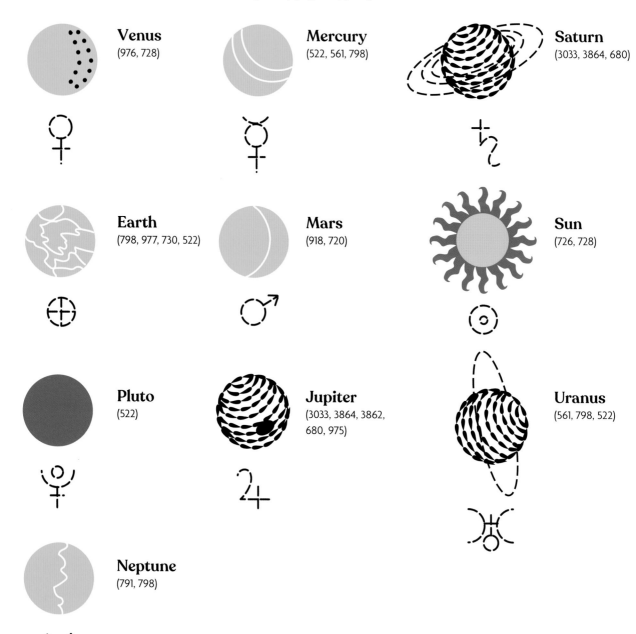

Venus
(976, 728)

Mercury
(522, 561, 798)

Saturn
(3033, 3864, 680)

Earth
(798, 977, 730, 522)

Mars
(918, 720)

Sun
(726, 728)

Pluto
(522)

Jupiter
(3033, 3864, 3862, 680, 975)

Uranus
(561, 798, 522)

Neptune
(791, 798)

Moon Phases

All moons are stitched using satin stitch and French knots or running stitch. The large moon is a combination of backstitch, running stitch, detached chain stitch, and seed stitch.

See Chapter 4, page 70, for symbols.

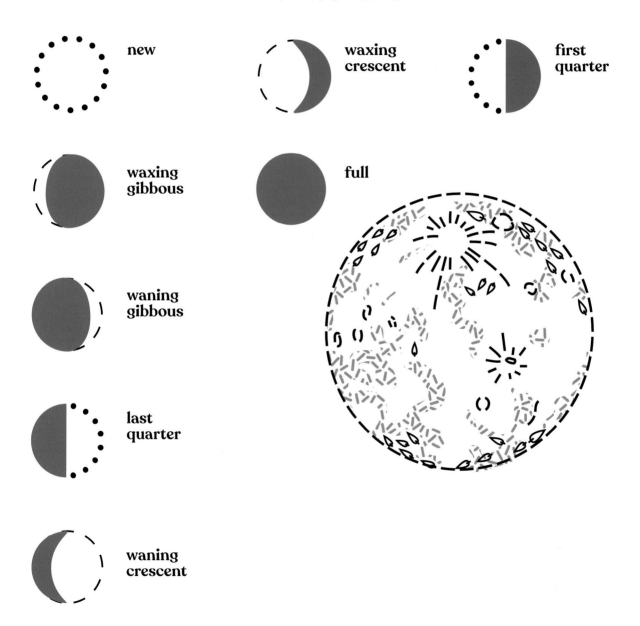

new

waxing crescent

first quarter

waxing gibbous

full

waning gibbous

last quarter

waning crescent

Zodiac Signs

See Chapter 4, page 72, for symbols.

The Zodiac

chain stitch wheel; backstitch interior spiral; three-strand backstitch zodiac signs; French knot on outer circle and galaxy; star stitch accents (779, 834, 3371, 3064, 647, 553)

Aries

backstitch outline of ram; fly stitch nose; satin stitch eyes; blanket stitch and backstitch edges of horns; French knots down nose; ray stitches on outside (975, 3371, 834)

Taurus

three-strand backstitch outline and blanket stitch horns; fly stitch interior V shapes; satin stitch back triangles; French knots on legs; detached chain stitch for eye (779, 728, 553)

Gemini

backstitch faces and arcs at top; fly stitch eyes; satin stitch hair; star stitch accents (553, 975, 728)

Cancer

satin stitch claws; star stitch eyes; satin stitch moons; double straight stitch for legs; backstitch base of body; accent shape with French knots (3064, 779, 3371)

Leo

satin stitch mane, eyes, nose, and ears; French knots at forehead; straight stitch whiskers and mouth (680, 839, 3852)

Virgo

chain stitch hair in alternating colors; satin stitch wheat and figure (680, 931, 829, 3371)

Libra

stem to satin stitch tree; chain stitch accent arcs; satin stitch bowls of scales; three-strand backstitch scale supports and roots; three-strand French knot details (829, 3852, 931, 975)

Scorpio

satin stitch body; straight stitch legs; star stitch and French knot accents (975, 931, 976)

Sagittarius

backstitch bow and arrow; satin stitch arrowhead; fly stitch arrow feathers; running stitch bow detail; star stitch and French knot accents (931, 612, 779)

Capricorn

backstitch two colors on outline; running stitch texture on tail; satin stitch horns and tail; detached chain stitch eye (with tiny straight stitch filling), straight stitch nose (976, 612, 3371)

Aquarius

chain stitch water; satin stitch vase and droplets; backstitch top edge of hand; two rows of backstitch for each vase handle (931, 3752, 976)

Pisces

three-strand backstitch outline; blanket stitch top fins; detached chain stitch eye; grid stitch scales on body; straight stitch tail; running stitch water (779, 3371, 931)

See Chapter 4, page 76, for symbols.

feather

satin stitch; stem stitch spine (834, 830, 3031)

moth or butterfly

satin stitch body and wings, using long and short stitch to blend two colors on upper wing; accent outer tips of upper wing and dashes on lower wing with tiny stitches covering satin stitch (950, 3064, 3371, 830, 834)

earthworm

satin stitch (3864, 3772, 844)

coral

top in French knot; bottom in feather stitch (3864, 3772)

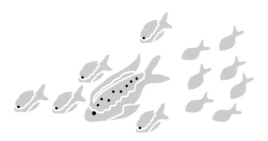

fish

long and short stitch, with French knots on top (3031, 451, 3852)

cowrie shell

satin stitch and backstitch (3770, 844)

owl

satin stitch head, tail, and wing; backstitch side of body; fill in chest with fly stitch (677, 3045, 3031)

hawk

Body and head: fill in with satin stitch; grid stitch over top of body; satin stitch eyes and straight stitch outline of nose, filling in beak with two small stitches; French knot on top of eyes. *Wings:* satin stitch feathers; three-strand straight stitch down middle of each feather (in the color of the row above it); chain stitch at top of wing. *Tail:* satin stitch rows of upper tail; backstitch zigzag at lower tail, alternating colors (728, 680, 829, 3371)

dove

Lightest color: satin stitch head; stem stitch top of wing; straight stitch ends of wings and tail. *Medium color:* satin stitch to fill in body and wings, overlapping with stitches of lighter color. *Darkest color:* alternate straight stitches with lightest color in wings and tail; French knots on body and eye; satin stitch beak; stem stitch top of wing (3862, 3864, 3371

egg

three-strand backstitch outline and cracking detail; satin stitch to fill in; French knot accents on top (3371, 677, 830)

raven

satin stitch body, tops of wing and tail, and head; backstitch around each feather; add three straight stitches for feet; fill in beak and eye with satin stitch; fill in each feather with a single straight stitch; overlap into upper satin stitch to blend colors (310, 333)

swan

All in three strands. *Darkest color:* backstitch outline; straight stitch beak and eye. *Next medium dark color:* add inner feathers of wing with detached chain stitch; accent body with running stitch. *Medium light color:* next row of feathers in detached chain stitch; backstitch ripples on water. *Lightest color:* next row of feathers in detached chain stitch (340, 341, 333, 791)

wing

satin stitch; chain stitch at top; outline in backstitch (950, 3064, 918)

bird claw

blanket stitch along one edge of each toe; backstitch opposite edge; fill in gaps with satin stitch; fly stitch toenails (3371, 680)

antler

satin stitch (834, 832)

nautilus

outline in three-strand split stitch; lines of inner chambers in backstitch (779)

oyster and pearl

satin stitch shell and pearl; chain stitch edge of shell (3064, 451, 779, 453)

conch

satin stitch, beginning with darkest areas and proceeding with each lighter shade (3770, 950, 3064, 918)

bee

three-strand backstitch wings and legs; satin stitch body; star stitch accents (728, 310, 645)

scarab

backstitch outline, legs, and antennae; satin stitch body, head, wings, and ball of dung; straight stitch edge of wings; split stitch to fill in stripes on wing covers (3371, 720, 830, 728)

spider

three-strand backstitch legs; satin stitch body; star stitch and French knot accents (310)

salamander

satin stitch body, adding shading with long and short stitch; top with French knots at sides and split stitch down spine (720, 918, 972)

serpent

satin stitch for long snake and circle snake; third snake is stem stitch (720, 677, 830)

wolf

Lightest color: fill in top edge of ears, head, and snout with satin stitch; straight stitch rays for cheeks. *Medium color:* fill in outer edge of ears, diamond at forehead, and upper eyebrows with satin stitch; fill in spaces between straight stitches of lighter color with smaller straight stitches; backstitch under mouth. *Darkest color:* backstitch outline of eyes, sides of nose, and mouth; fill in ears, nose, eyebrows, and middle of eyes with satin stitch; fill in color of iris with small satin stitches (648, 645, 3799, 726)

bear

satin stitch claws; three-strand chain stitch pad of paw in alternating stripes (975, 3371)

ant

French knots for body; two-strand straight stitch for legs (3371)

big cats

satin stitch and straight stitch dark stripes; stem stitch at top edge of head; starting with darkest color, fill in remainder with long and short stitch, following lines separating sections of colors (834, 680, 830, 310)

stingray

three-strand backstitch and running stitch for outline, spine, eyes, and tail; seed stitch for shading (645)

octopus

three-strand backstitch and French knots (779)

mouse

satin stitch body and head; split stitch tail; three-strand straight stitch legs and toes (610)

rabbit
three-strand backstitch (3031)

deer
All in three strands. *Darkest color:* satin stitch eye. *Medium color:* backstitch outline; satin stitch nose; straight stitch fur at chest and shading under neck. *Lightest color:* straight stitch details of fur texture (610, 612, 3031)

frog
satin stitch body; straight stitch toes; one tiny stitch for dark of eye (166, 469, 3031)

sea turtle
Lightest color: chain stitch around edge of shell; satin stitch to fill in top of each shell motif. *Medium color:* fill in lower area of each shell motif; straight stitch to outline these shapes. *Darkest color:* satin stitch head and legs; backstitch around outer edge of light-colored chain stitch; blanket stitch inner edge of light-colored chain stitch, with each leg of blanket stitch going over chain stitch and meeting backstitch on outer edge (500, 520, 3013)

elephant
All in three strands. *Darkest color:* backstitch outline, tail, and edge of saddle; satin stitch eye. *Accent color 1 (clay):* star stitches on trunk; ray stitch at eye; straight stitches on ear; blanket stitch on saddle. *Accent color 2 (lime):* star stitch on legs; fly stitch on saddle and face. *Accent color 3 (emerald):* French knots and detached chain stitch on saddle; backstitch curlicue on ear and crown on head, with French knots surrounding crown. *Accent color 4 (tan):* satin stitch tusks and toenails (3031, 301, 166, 500, 612)

Mythical Beasts

See Chapter 4, page 85, for symbols.

phoenix

Darkest color: backstitch outline of body, head, wings, and feathers (including ends of tail feathers); three-strand fly stitch and backstitch for lines connecting tail feathers to body; satin stitch beak. After finishing all stitches of next two colors, go back with this color to fill in V shapes on body with satin stitch. *Lightest color:* detached chain stitch on upper part of each feather (including ends of tail feathers); straight stitch V shapes on body; satin stitch to fill in feathers on top of head. After finishing with medium color, go back in with detached chain stitch for eye. *Medium color:* straight stitches to fill in remainder of feathers (one on each side of the detached chain stitch, ending in a V shape); straight stitches on body inside V shapes of lightest color, satin stitch head; remember to go back in with detached chain stitch for eye in lightest color, and fill in V shapes with darkest color (918, 301, 726)

winged horse

Darkest color: backstitch outline of body; fly stitch tail; chain stitch saddle and top of wing; satin stitch head; French knots above head. *Accent color 1 (clay):* chain stitch outer mane stripes; backstitch stripes on neck; French knot around saddle; satin stitch wings. *Accent color 2 (lavender):* fill in remaining space at mane and neck with chain stitch and backstitch; shade body with running stitch. *Accent color 3 (yellow):* satin stitch wing; detached chain stitch eye (340, 301, 3031, 728)

sphinx

three-strand backstitch outline and details; chain stitch alternating colors for headcloth (610, 728)

unicorn

three-strand backstitch outline; satin stitch eye; satin stitch horn and hair (728, 340, 610)

dragon

Lightest color: chain stitch belly side of body from neck to tail; add a second row of chain stitch to thicker section from chest to bottom of belly, tapering ends; stem stitch tail. *Medium color:* chain stitch from top of head all the way to curve of tail, keeping stitch close to previous chain stitches. Fill in head with satin stitch, and upper half of wings with long and short stitch. *Darkest color:* satin stitch beak; chain stitch from top of head to curve of tail, keeping close to previous stitches; outline tail with backstitch; switch to blanket stitch to outline front of body; outline wings, ears, and face with backstitch. *Accent color (lavender):* fill in remainder of wings using long and short stitch; fill in ears with detached chain stitch (340, 726, 166, 520)

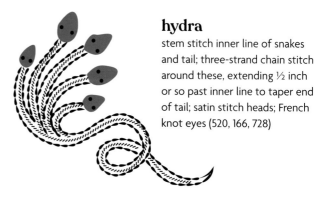

hydra

stem stitch inner line of snakes and tail; three-strand chain stitch around these, extending ½ inch or so past inner line to taper end of tail; satin stitch heads; French knot eyes (520, 166, 728)

griffin

Darkest color: three-strand outline body, wings, V shapes on body, and face details. *Medium color:* running stitch texture on lower body; fill in claws with two straight stitches for each finger; straight stitch on inside edge of V shapes at chest; satin stitch head and tuft on tail; chain stitch top of wing and outermost feathers, with detached chain stitch for smaller feathers close to body. *Light color:* satin stitch beak and feathers at back of head; straight stitch inside of V shapes at chest; detached chain stitch to fill in small wing feathers (680, 726, 3371)

Botanica

See Chapter 4, page 87, for symbols.

root
three-strand backstitch (829)

apple
satin stitch seeds and stem; chain stitch to fill in flesh of apple; stem stitch around this in consecutively darker shades for skin of apple (3371, 3770, 758, 718)

seed
satin stitch (3371)

wheat
detached chain stitches filled in with straight stitch; backstitch stem (3045, 677)

sage
satin stitch and stem stitch (3347, 3013, 934)

mushroom
straight stitch grass; long and short stitch caps; satin stitch stem; French knots on top of satin stitch (520, 552, 333, 553, 3770, 829)

marigold
satin stitch base of flower; stem stitch stem and spine of leaves; three-strand detached chain stitch leaves; stem stitch shadow of stem and texture on base of flower; satin stitch petals; outline each petal in three-strand backstitch (469, 934, 972, 975)

calendula
detached chain stitch petals; single straight stitch for highlight in middle of each petal; single straight stitch for shadows in between petals (near middle of flower); French knot to fill in center; diagonal satin stitch for stem and leaf, with stem stitch highlight at center of leaf (728, 726, 830, 3852, 470)

dandelion

straight stitch petals and seeds; chain stitch stem; satin stitch leaves (444, 733, 581)

red clover

seed stitch petals, topped with tiny 1/8-inch-long three-strand straight stitch; stem stitch beneath flowers; satin stitch leaves (554, 3770, 718, 3347)

rosemary

stem stitch (3362)

mugwort

three-strand chain stitch, starting with lightest color on inside (677, 3363, 3362)

lily

satin stitch outer petals; long and short stitch center petal; straight stitch stamen; satin stitch leaves and stem (3770, 758, 934, 730)

goldenrod

detached chain stitch flowers; split stitch stems; satin stitch leaves (728, 733)

yarrow

French knot flowers; three-strand backstitch upper stems; three-strand chain stitch lower stems; three-strand fly stitch leaves (758, 730)

poppy

long and short stitch petals; satin stitch center; stem stitch stem; satin stitch leaves and seedpod (977, 720, 934, 728, 522)

rose

inner petals in satin stitch; outer petals in long and short stitch; French knots at center (758, 720, 918, 934)

peony

satin stitch inner petals; chain stitch inner outline; long and short stitch outer petals; stem stitch stems; satin stitch leaves (3770, 977, 720, 934, 522)

iris

flower is made of rows of three-strand chain stitch, starting with a single row of accent color at center of petals; surround with single row of palest shade; repeat with next two darkest shades; with darkest color, satin stitch to fill in remaining petal shape, and backstitch upper petals; leaves are a mix of stem stitch and satin stitch, with a satin stitch bulb (728, 341, 340, 333, 791, 469, 934, 522)

snapdragon

each flower is made of two detached chain stitches with beginning of stitches close together; split stitch stem; satin stitch leaves (718, 730)

mandrake

satin stitch leaves; long and short stitch root; outline in backstitch (3362, 934, 976, 975, 3031)

thistle

petals are four fly stitches close together; base of flower is grid stitch outlined in backstitch; stem is split stitch; leaves are satin stitch (553, 3362, 522)

borage

Flowers: French knot center of flowers; straight stitch V shapes of each petal; continue to fill in with V shapes in each consecutively lighter color; straight stitch in between each petal in accent color. *Stems and leaves:* satin stitch at a diagonal angle, with two fly stitches for base of buds. *Buds:* fill in center of fly stitches with two straight stitches in flower color; in accent color, make three straight stitches that join at tip (333, 340, 341, 718, 522, 3362)

pineapple

Medium color: fly stitch each V shape, filling in any gaps in outline with backstitch. *Light color:* inside these V shapes, add two diagonal rows of straight stitch to fill in. *Green:* add foliage at top using long detached chain stitches. *Dark color:* fill in foliage with single straight stitch, fill in points of V shapes with French knot (830, 3852, 470, 934)

pomegranate

satin stitch leaves and seeds; long and short stitch fruit; in darkest color, three-strand backstitch interior opening of fruit; three-strand straight stitch details at tips of fruit; three-strand chain stitch stem (561, 3347, 918, 356, 758, 677, 3031)

bamboo
satin stitch (733, 469, 934)

palm
satin stitch leaves and center;
backstitch down center of leaves
(166, 469, 3819)

saguaro cactus
stem stitch outline and stripes on
inside; chain stitch to fill in gaps
on inside (561, 3013)

lotus
satin stitch (948, 758, 356, 3347)

cedar
split stitch stems; straight stitch
leaves (470)

bay laurel
satin stitch leaves; stem stitch
stem (3013, 3347, 830)

juniper
feather stitch leaves; satin stitch
berries (500, 504)

white pine
stem stitch for branches;
detached chain stitch for
pinecone filled in with small
straight stitches; three-strand
stem stitch for pine needles (832,
830, 3347)

oak
backstitch veins at center; satin
stitch to fill in leaf (975, 680)

maple
backstitch veins at center; satin
stitch to fill in leaf (3371, 301)

Forces of Nature

See Chapter 4, page 94, for symbols.

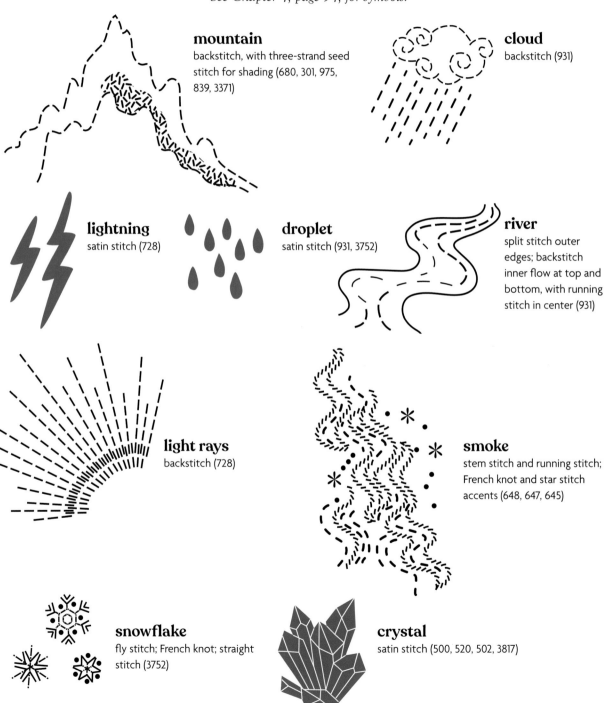

mountain
backstitch, with three-strand seed stitch for shading (680, 301, 975, 839, 3371)

cloud
backstitch (931)

lightning
satin stitch (728)

droplet
satin stitch (931, 3752)

river
split stitch outer edges; backstitch inner flow at top and bottom, with running stitch in center (931)

light rays
backstitch (728)

smoke
stem stitch and running stitch; French knot and star stitch accents (648, 647, 645)

snowflake
fly stitch; French knot; straight stitch (3752)

crystal
satin stitch (500, 520, 502, 3817)

Human Forms

See Chapter 4, page 97, for symbols.

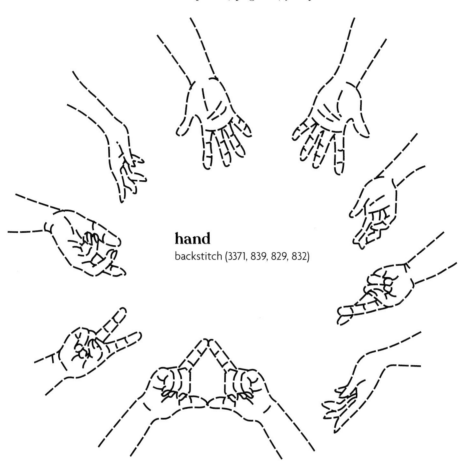

hand
backstitch (3371, 839, 829, 832)

eye
three-strand backstitch outer rays;
satin stitch lashes, moon, and inner
filling of iris; backstitch dark outline
of eye; three rows of chain stitch
around iris in consecutively darker
shades (3852, 712, 798, 310, 791)

ear
three-strand backstitch (3371)

mouth

satin stitch (356)

teeth

satin stitch to fill in; three-strand backstitch for outline and shading details (677, 3371)

tongue

backstitch outline; fill in with chain stitch (779, 758)

skull

backstitch outline and teeth; satin stitch eye and nose cavities (779)

hair

stem to satin stitch loose hair; satin stitch braid (677, 3045)

heart

backstitch blue veins; fill in heart with satin stitch (be sure not to cover up backstitch veins); fill in all upper arteries with satin stitch (798, 720, 918, 779, 3772, 758)

foot

satin stitch (610)

lungs

backstitch veins; satin stitch to fill in around backstitch (758, 918, 720)

Our Tools

See Chapter 4, page 100, for symbols.

candle

chain stitch; backstitch smoke and around flame; accent smoke with running stitch; French knots and star stitch for accents (645, 728, 677, 610, 612)

vase

Medium color: backstitch outline of vase body and two stripes at widest point; straight stitch vertical stripes at top and bottom; chain stitch handles, opening, base (2 rows), and stripe above zigzag row. *Light color:* chain stitch interior opening (at top); backstitch horizontal stripes; fill in vertical stripes at top with straight stitch; satin stitch upper triangles of zigzag row. *Darkest color:* chain stitch to fill in opening at top; backstitch remaining horizontal stripes; satin stitch lower triangles of zigzag row; fill in vertical stripes at bottom with straight stitch (3045, 3371, 677)

rope

wrapped double chain stitch: two chain stitches made as close together as possible, then wrapped with contrast color (612, 839)

wand

long and short stitch for stick; ray stitch (839, 612)

comb

satin stitch (839, 612)

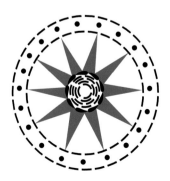

wheel

satin stitch triangular spokes; backstitch outline; accent with French knots. Interior circle is, from center moving out: one row of dark backstitch, one row of light backstitch, one row of medium backstitch, one row of light backstitch, and one row of dark chain stitch (728, 612, 3371)

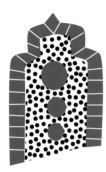

door

satin stitch doorframe and circles on inside; French knot texture inside door (779, 340, 728, 680)

key

three-strand chain stitch (340)

stairs or ladder

backstitch, with running stitch for shading (779)

pyramid

chain stitch stripes; satin stitch top (680, 728)

bowl

Dark color: backstitch outline and top edge; fly stitch shadows of gems. *Medium color:* chain stitch top rim; satin stitch body of bowl, alternating stitches with light color. *Light color:* chain stitch interior of bowl; fill in remaining body of bowl with satin stitch. *Gem color:* satin stitch to fill in fly stitch in dark color (3371, 680, 728, 340)

sword

satin stitch blade and end of handle; chain stitch handle guard; split stitch stripes on handle; straight stitch cross at end of handle; outline end of handle in backstitch (648, 645, 728)

labyrinth

backstitch (770)

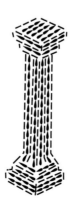

pillar

outline in backstitch; fill in with chain stitch (829, 677)

broom

satin stitch handle at a diagonal; long and short stitch straw of broom; backstitch stripes on broom; add ⅛-inch straight stitches to bottom to indicate shading (610, 834)

temple

satin stitch stairs and roof; backstitch outline; fill in walls with alternating rows of chain stitch (3852, 726, 779, 340)

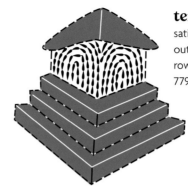

coin

fill with long and short stitch; edge is satin stitch in alternating colors (680, 3371)

mask

three-strand backstitch (839)

chain

chain stitch; outline with three-strand backstitch (834, 830)

hourglass

three-strand backstitch outline of glass; fill with French knot for sand; chain stitch five rows in alternating colors at either end (646, 975, 3852)

chalice

Cup from top to bottom: chain stitch top rim; satin stitch in alternating colors; chain stitch; French knots in red, fill in gaps with satin stitch; chain stitch. *Circle:* backstitch outline, fill in with satin stitch. *Base:* 5 detached chain stitches in gold; satin stitch; 4 rows backstitch; 1 row chain stitch (728, 680, 839, 720)

knot

chain stitch; outline with backstitch (918, 720)

TRANSCENDENT TALISMAN

Ouroboros of Transformation
See page 118

Scarab of Abundance
See page 120

Portal to the Unknown
See page 122

The Heart That Grows
See page 126

Love Flows Freely
See page 124

Galactic Denim Jeans
See page 134

Fortune's Conjure Jacket
See page 140

Visionary Denim Shirt
See page 138

Transcendent Talisman Patterns

Ouroboros of Transformation

Scarab of Abundance

Portal to the Unknown

Love Flows Freely

The Heart That Grows

Galactic Denim Jeans

Cosmic stardust

Planet/ring

Snake

Galactic mist

Large star

Moon

Enlarge pattern 225%

Visionary Denim Shirt

Rays

Eye

Fortune's Conjure Jacket

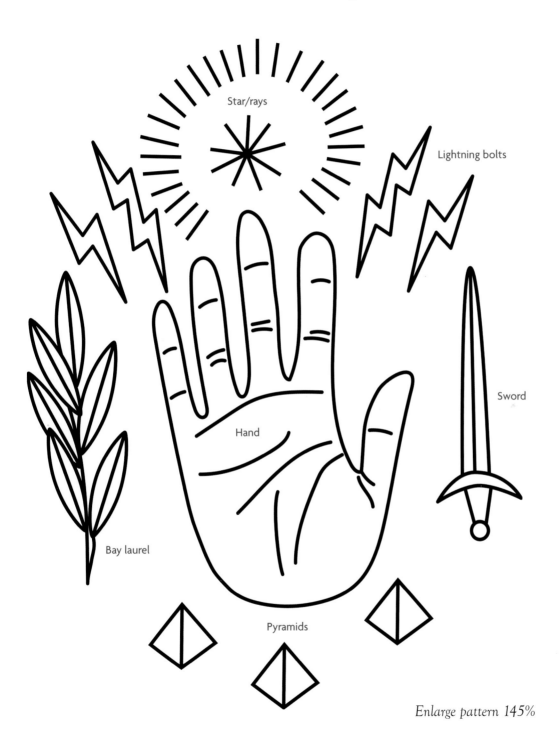

Star/rays

Lightning bolts

Sword

Hand

Bay laurel

Pyramids

Enlarge pattern 145%

Resources

Though I can't travel back in time to figure out exactly which library books of my youth lit my creative fire so brightly, I do know my current collection of publications has been extremely supportive in the creation of this book. Here are the books that served as either reference or inspiration for this book.

Creativity

May, Rollo. *The Courage to Create*. Norton and Company, 1994.

Newport, Cal. *Deep Work*. Grand Central Publishing, 2016.

Wolf, Guillaume. *You Are a Dream*. CreateSpace Independent Publishing, 2017.

Embroidery

Alfers, Betty. *Creative Crewel*. Grosset and Dunlap, 1970.

Day, Lewis F., and Mary Buckle. *Art Nouveau Embroidery*. Discovery House, 1974.

Howard, Constance. *Inspiration for Embroidery*. B. T. Batsford, 1967.

Jacopetti, Alexandra. *Native Funk & Flash*. Scrimshaw Press, 1974.

Meilach, Dona Z. *Creative Stitchery*. Reilly & Lee, 1970.

Snook, Barbara. *The Creative Art of Embroidery*. Hamlyn, 1972.

Snook, Barbara. *Needlework Stitches*. Literary Licensing, 2012.

Wilson, Erica. *Embroidery Book*. Charles Scribner's Sons, 1973.

Herbalism

Bennett, Robin Rose. *The Gift of Healing Herbs*. North Atlantic Books, 2014.

Beyerl, Paul. *The Master Book of Herbalism*. Phoenix Publishing, 1984.

Cunningham, Scott. *Encyclopedia of Magical Herbs*. Llewellyn Publications, 1985.

Gladstar, Rosemary. *Herbal Recipes for Vibrant Health*. Storey, 2008.

Müller-Ebeling, Claudia, Christian Rätsch, and Wolf-Dieter Storl. *Witchcraft Medicine*. Inner Traditions, 2003.

Popham, Sajah. *Evolutionary Herbalism*. North Atlantic Books, 2019.

Pursell, J. J. *The Herbal Apothecary*. Timber Press, 2015.

Roth, Harold. *The Witching Herbs*. Weiser Books, 2017.

Toll, Maia. *The Illustrated Herbiary*. Storey, 2018.

Metaphysical

Benson, Herbert, and Miriam Z. Klipper. *The Relaxation Response*. HarperCollins, 2009.

González-Wippler, Migene. *The Complete Book of Amulets and Talismans*. Llewellyn Publications, 1991.

Lundy, Miranda, Anthony Ashton, Jason Martineau, Daud Sutton, and John Martineau. *Quadrivium*. Wooden Books, 2010.

Whitehurst, Tess. *Holistic Energy Magic*. Llewellyn Publications, 2015.

Patterns

To download traceable patterns for all the symbols and projects in this book, visit www.storey.com/symbol-patterns/.

Symbolism

Banzhaf, Hajo. *The Crowley Tarot*. U.S. Games, 2000.

Campbell, Joseph. *The Inner Reaches of Outer Space*. New World Library, 2012.

Campbell, Joseph. *The Mythic Image*. Princeton University Press, 1981.

Cavendish, Richard. *Mythology: An Illustrated Encyclopedia*. Fall Rivers Press, 1992.

Cooper, J. C. *An Illustrated Encyclopaedia of Traditional Symbols*. Thames & Hudson, 1987.

Gimbutas, Marija Alseikaite. *The Language of the Goddess*. HarperCollins, 1991.

Hickey, Isabel M. *Astrology: A Cosmic Science*. CRCS Publications, 2011.

Acknowledgments

Huxley, Francis. *The Way of the Sacred*. Aldus Books, 1974.

Johnson, Buffie. *Lady of the Beasts*. Inner Traditions, 1994.

Jung, Carl G. *Man and His Symbols*. Dell Publishing, 1968.

Klossowski de Rola, Stanislas. *Alchemy: The Secret Art*. Thames & Hudson, 2013.

Tresidder, Jack. *Dictionary of Symbols*. Chronicle, 1998.

A huge and forever thank-you to both of my parents for nurturing my creative spirit. Extra special thanks to my mother for spending her free time showing me how to make everything from tie-dye T-shirts to life-size papier-mâché monsters—and perhaps more so, for teaching me that I could teach myself more than I could possibly imagine. Thank you to my sister, Akina, for being the one I could talk to about jumping into new and unknown territory, and always being there to say "Yes! Go for it!"; and to my brother, Greg, for all his attempts to help me build a thick skin (though they all failed).

Thank you to my love, Nicholas, for making me meals and making sure the fire was blazing and the chickens were safe in the coop each night while I shouted "Did you feed the cat yet?" from my studio, covered in embroidery floss and buried in old books—and for always pushing me to make something better, even when it meant more meals needed preparing. Also, thanks to Tiger the cat for being the sweetest, fluffiest ball of love and support.

Thank you to Stacey Wakefield Forte for telling me more than once that I should turn my humble zine into a book proposal, and then holding my hand through actually putting it together because I was clearly not going to do it myself. Thank you to Natalie Ross of Earth Speak, who made it possible to think I could even make a zine in the first place. Thank you to Haley Ann Bradley and Cheryl Humphreys for teaching me the ways of InDesign and for so much other graphic design education, and to John Moore for allowing us all to explore art and design while working in an inspiring space. Thank you to Pamela Mayer, Allison Knowland Ward, and Kim Krans for indulging in my monthly meetings to keep us all doing the best we could. Thank you to Karen Morris for helping me see the ways I held myself back; and thank you to Jessica Adamson, my fabulous "stitchsistant," for making it happen when I just couldn't stitch another stitch.

Last, but certainly not least, eternal thanks to my grandmothers—though they never taught me how to sew, their lifetime of skills was passed down nonetheless—and to my aunts Minnie, Lynn, and Laurie who continue to encourage my creative pursuits in stitches.

Index